Brewing a Creative Culture

by
The Staff of
Dillanos Coffee Roasters

Bloomington, IN Milton Keynes, UK

authorHOUSE™

AuthorHouse™
1663 Liberty Drive, Suite 200
Bloomington, IN 47403
www.authorhouse.com
Phone: 1-800-839-8640

AuthorHouse™ UK Ltd.
500 Avebury Boulevard
Central Milton Keynes, MK9 2BE
www.authorhouse.co.uk
Phone: 08001974150

First published by AuthorHouse 12/26/07

ISBN: 1-4208-3392-8 (dj)
ISBN: 1-4208-3309-X (sc)

Printed in the United States of America
Bloomington, Indiana

This book is printed on acid-free paper.

Table of Contents

 # Foreword

By Lon LaFlamme

What comes from the heart goes to the heart.
- Charles Chaplin

When Dillanos' CEO, David Morris, asked me to scratch out some introductory thoughts for a booklet about the company's culture, I knew it would be easy. Dillanos' culture is so dramatically different from the companies I had worked for in the past.

Besides leading a marketing communications company for many years, I worked on strategic planning and marketing at the CEO/management-committee level in more than twenty industries. But I never found work to be an adventure until I started sharing my life with Dillanos Coffee Roasters.

There are more than 1,200 specialty coffee roasters in America; many with names far better known than Dillanos. Although Dillanos has customers in nearly every state including Alaska and Hawaii, wholesalers are not usually listed with their customers' brand names. And after working with Starbucks' Chairman,

Howard Schultz, I wondered what a growing little micro roaster could teach me about management.

Everything.

As a self-published novelist, I flinch at the idea of diving into an ocean of blank pages. This project was different. Although I have only been working for the company for three years, I feel like I am writing about a lifetime friend.

Let's start by getting to the core of Dillanos: Family. Co-founder, David Morris, and his stepfather and Chairman of the Board, Howard Heyer, along with David's stepbrother and President, Chris Heyer, make every employee feel like a member of the family.

My journey with Dillanos, as with every employee, is as much a journey of the heart and soul as it is of carving out a way to live seven days a week. Besides serving as CEO, David also energizes the company as creative director and head cheerleader.

There isn't a day that goes by when he doesn't rush into my office like Kramer on television's Seinfeld, wide-eyed and possessed by an idea he just has to get out right now.

<u>Right now</u> is what David and Dillanos are all about. Not that the "The Power of Now" doesn't have its downsides, as bands of employees madly rush to make possible the impossible because of seemingly insane time frames. You'll sometimes hear a bit of grumbling by new employees who are amazed by expectations. But in less than a month, they understand that Dillanos isn't a job, it's an adventure. And if they still don't fit into this creative culture, they tend to leave on their own, preserving Dillanos' unique environment.

After just weeks of working with the company, I noticed that there was no fear of heights. Everyone's commitment to the one- to three-year sales mission we all help define and strive to fulfill never waivers. Management is always exploring new sales channels and opportunities of all sizes. When a new project doesn't work, we go back to the drawing board and are off on another adventure, often accepting an ounce of risk for a pound of reward and a ton of fun.

So how could we harness the multitude of things that collectively define Dillanos? As we gathered ideas, I realized it would be impossible to create a blueprint for brewing a creative culture that small business owners can follow step-by-step. The authors deliver a wealth of ideas, many of which you can adapt immediately, regardless of your industry. But the book doesn't offer cookie-cutter solutions. How you foster a creative culture must be as unique as you.

Having employees write about the Dillanos adventure in their own words symbolizes the company culture. I have tried to keep the writers' spirit and sincerity. The book will transport you into the minds and lives of employees ranging from our roast master to the executive assistant and a delivery driver. Each of them captures what makes the business unique and enables it to sustain its skyrocketing growth. So start reading and join the adventure called Dillanos.

 Introduction

By David J. Morris & Chris Heyer

At the moment of commitment, the world conspires to assist you.
- Tyler Gordon

The idea for the staff to write a book was developed with one central concept: Protect Dillanos' culture. As each staff member brought their stories and suggestions to life on paper, we realized our customers, potential customers and even company owners outside the coffee industry could find take-away value in the book.

As you read, you may think this too-good-to-be-true company has to be more fable than fact. You would be right. Nobody's perfect. We wish we could say that we live the book's principles 24/7. But we have tripped, stumbled and taken two steps back for one step forward in following every formula for blending outrageous fun with high accountability.

What you will read is heartfelt and we have tried to get each author's thoughts down in an easy-to-read format you will enjoy.

We are aware of our daily failures, but they don't tarnish the staff's spirit. They believe every word they have written. Despite our shortcomings, the values and mission statement we all attempt to live by have contributed to creating a company everybody loves. If your company's culture isn't like ours, take heart. A clear focus and a sincere intent to follow these formulas will lead to huge personal and professional rewards.

1

Dare To Be Real

Jay Lijewski, Dillanos National Sales Representative

Better to have heart without words - than words without heart.
- Anonymous

Formula 1:

Hire from the heart for the heart.

Sometimes the slightest, smallest thing can change someone's life. It could be a teacher, or it could be a song. For a lot of people, it may be a relative. It just may be a book that could make all the difference in the world. I don't know that I can say that it was this book alone that changed my life, but I can assure you that without this book, I may not be where I am today. And I can hardly put into words where I am today, so let's start with yesterday.

The following story took place around the time when the first printing of this book was released in 2005. I was one of the first people to take what this book had to say to heart. The outcome is still talked about today, two and half years later...

So, there I was, managing a café in Tacoma, WA. At that point, I had been a barista for eight years, and the coffee we were using was the best that I had ever used. It was consistently fresh and smooth. That was a given. Here in the Pacific Northwest, good coffee is not too hard to find. Even though I only had brief glimpses of it, there was something magic, way beyond roasting coffee going on with our vendor. I felt it instantly whenever crossing paths with our roaster's staff at any level.

That something was a culture. That roaster was Dillanos. And

I wanted in. Right now!

One day at the café, as I was doing my thing behind the machine, my delivery driver walked in with my coffee order. His name was John Berg (you will get to know John in Chapter 9 of this book). On a whim, I asked John if there were any open positions at Dillanos.

"Yeah, actually we are looking for another sales rep!" he said while putting our coffee away in the cupboard.

That was exactly what I wanted to hear. My sales representative was Anna Gutierrez and I was so envious of her job. She was always in a great mood. She traveled a lot for work, and she had a deeper link to the coffee industry than I had as a barista. I immediately called Anna to ask her if what John had told me was true. She said that it was indeed true, and that I should email my resume to her, and she would personally give it to her manager. That was the first thing I did when I got home.

Well, I went right home and crafted a brief resume. A few days later I got a call from Jeff Woods, the sales manager at Dillanos. Before the conversation was over, he invited me in to the roaster for an interview.

Holy crap! This was my shot. I was about to get a dream job! After about five minutes of jumping up and down and giving myself high fives, I started to think about the type of person that they would want to hire. Responsible. Professional. Polished. These had to be the three main traits that jumped out to me that Dillanos wanted in a sales rep. My sales rep was all that, and a lot more.

I was about to lose out on this incredible opportunity for one reason: I was not letting my true self shine through.

I went shopping for responsible and professional clothes. I bought slacks. I bought black, shiny shoes. I bought a couple of nice crisp shirts, and even a few ties. No more kid stuff! I was going after a serious job here.

The morning of my interview, I put those new slacks on, laced up those new shoes and…uh…. learned how to tie that tie! Oh man, was I looking like a professional, or what?

When I arrived at Dillanos, the first thing I did was head straight for the bathroom, just to make sure that my tie was straight and my fly was up. I got so nervous because my shirt got a little wrinkly from the drive to the roaster. " Oh, they are not going to like this," I thought.

When I sat down in the lobby waiting for Jeff, I noticed that everyone there was wearing jeans and t-shirts. I even saw a guy wearing shorts and flip-flops. (I later found out that he was the CEO). So, I was feeling a little over dressed. Everyone was looking at me like I was about to sell him or her some pre-paid legal services or an insurance policy.

I shook that off and stayed focused on driving home the fact that I am a very mature, responsible professional. Just as I was taking my last sip of coffee that I got from the lobby, Jeff arrived, ready to take me to his office for the interview. I was composed. I was ready to shine. I was a professional, and very, very responsible. A perfect fit for what looked and felt like a perfect company from the second my toes crossed the threshold of the lobby doors.

> It is important to hire individuals and let them grow into their own person. Thus, allowing the company itself to become more diverse.

About halfway through the interview their vice president, Keith Hayward walked in. He chatted with me a bit with what I later learned as his best poker face, and then walked out. The interview was a marathon, about three hours long! I felt that I drove my point home. You know, about being a respons… Aw never mind, you already know by now.

At the end of the interview, Jeff took in a deep breath, sat back in his chair and looked me in the eye. He said, "Look Jay, I have no doubt that you would do a great job, and I would never have to worry about you dropping the ball. I just don't think that

you would fit in to our culture. I mean, you just seem a little....
tight, and we like to have a good time here while getting the job
done."

That's when it hit me like a Mack truck head on. I was about
to lose out on this incredible opportunity for one reason: I was not
letting my true self shine through. While I had genuinely grown
into a responsible person, I wasn't being myself. I was acting like a
robot, not a human. It was slipping away right in front of my eyes!
I had to do something.

"Wait! Jeff, I just learned how to tie this tie this morning! I
don't even like these pants, AND this starch is giving me a rash! I
just thought that this was the type of person that you would want
to hire. You know, kind of a corporate guy." I inhaled like I was taking my last breath. "I thought I'd give that a shot."

> When a culture is strong and defined, it will always attract people of like mind and heart.

Jeff paused and seemed to look right down to my soul.

"Okay," Jeff said, slowly nodding his head. "I will bring you back in for a second interview. But, I want you to read something before you come
back." He leaned over to his bookshelf and threw me a copy of the
first printing of the book in your hands right now.

"Read this. It will help you understand what we are looking for. We do things a little differently here. This book will explain our culture, because it was written by all of us."

I took this very book home and treated it like a homework assignment. I treated it like required college reading, a prerequisite. And it was just that, until I started to read it.

I wasn't too many pages in when I realized what I was reading could only come straight from the heart of Dillanos staff, not the marketing department, as one may suspect.

It was raw. It was real. It struck a chord in me like no book I have ever read before. It no longer felt like a hurdle that I had to jump in order to get a job. It felt like a life lesson. The authors were talking about the importance of hiring individuals and letting them grow into their own person at work. Thus, allowing the company itself to become more and more diverse -- AND effective! *Brewing a Creative Culture* illustrated the amazing things that can happen when there is a common goal that all employees can understand, as well as work towards.

This book painted such an incredible picture of Dillanos and the community under its roof that I began to understand how large of a mistake I had made by trying to be something that I wasn't. Could there really be a company out there that not only supported, but also celebrated individuality? I did not know how to be a corporate clone. I did not know how to act like the tie-wearing stereotype. Now I got it!

I had attempted to fake it in my first interview with Jeff and he instantly felt it. Therefore, my efforts to prove my worth to the company fell way short. I also came to the understanding that by me trying to hide my true self while showing them something I wasn't, I was doing everyone at Dillanos a huge disservice. It was actually very disrespectful to an incredibly unique culture that they had carefully created and EVERYBODY protected like a mother protects her young. What was I thinking?

"Could there really be a place that not only allows an individual room to grow his or her own way, but that actually awards it?" I thought to myself.

"Okay, I am all in!" I had nothing to lose! Why not get crazy? I had to find ways to show all ten people that were going to be in my second interview exactly who I was, and let them know how much I bought in to everything in this book.

That's right, I said TEN PEOPLE! I found out exactly who would be in the interview. Jeff would be there, along with Keith and Scott (the VPs), David and Chris (CEO and President), Celeste and Julie (David's wife and Chris's wife), Patti and Howard (David and Chris's parents) and possibly Lon (head of Marketing). It felt more like a potential family adoption than a job interview. I was suddenly petrified.

I started thinking of all of the things that I could do in order to let my true personality be known. I rehearsed over and over in my mind, what I would say.

"Well, I just read a book about all of these people. I don't have a book about myself, but what I do have is a photo album!" I wanted to bring along my entire CD collection, because you can tell a lot about someone by the type of music they listen to.

The position that I was trying to land was a different job than I had ever done before, so I needed to find a way to convey the fact that I can pick up on things rather quickly. A couple of months prior to this interview, I began to play the banjo and I thought I was grasping that pretty quickly. Then I would really grab them and say, " I wrote Dillanos a song based on the emotions that I felt while reading about this company." I was getting more and more wide-eyed. "I can use all three chords that I know too! It'll be great!"

Was I going too far? Would I be left the lonely fool, stuck in front of a ton of people? I wanted them desperately to know the real me that was starting to emerge as soon as I finished

Don't be afraid to open your heart and let people know all of the little things. You'd be amazed by the connections you can forge.

Brewing a Creative Culture. Then again, I was planning this out a lot like Jackson Pollock planned his canvases, with emotion and crazy as hell!

The night before the big day, I had a couple of good friends over to talk about everything that I had planned, and was prepared to do in order to land this job. After I walked them through my plan, they looked at each other then looked at me like I had a third arm sprouting out of my neck.

They said, "Jay, we understand what you are trying to do, but the last thing that you should do is make a mockery of what they do there. They're not crazy, or they wouldn't be doing so well. Just be you this time. Don't make yourself look like a circus clown!"

"Yeah, maybe you guys are right. All of that does seem a little much for an interview." And on that note, they left and I climbed into bed.

As I lay there trying to fall asleep, I kept thinking about the things that I had planned, the song I wrote for them and how I felt more like myself when I was doing those things. If I go in there and don't do everything that I wanted to do in that interview, and I don't get the job, would I forever be wondering, "What if?"

Furthermore, if I go there and do exactly what my gut was telling me to do and don't get the job, well, then they weren't the right fit for me! Maybe I want to interview them for a position in my life.

I was going to do it my way.

So, I woke up in the morning and I loaded up my photo album, with no picture left out either! I won't take you there, but let's just say, uh, that was a risky call. But, I wanted to give them the clearest idea of who they could potentially be hiring. I had decided to open my soul to these guys like I had never done before. I loaded up my CD books and banjo and hit the road. That's when the nerves hit.

The person who gets the farthest is generally the one who is willing to do and dare. The sure-thing boat never gets far from shore.

I kept thinking about how many people were going to be there.

"I need some kind of ice breaker," I said aloud to my car, obviously needing someone to talk to. I decided to roll into a drugstore on the way to see what kind of gifts I could pick up.

Right there on aisle four were little jelly bean dispensers shaped like various barnyard animals.

"They dispense brown jelly beans through their asses! Perfect!!" Yep, I was losing it.

I bought ten of them.

I walked into the lobby of Dillanos looking like a lunatic with my arms full of stuff, complete with a banjo on my back. It looked like they were wrapping up another interview in the big room on the other side of the beautiful two-way fireplace that greets you when you walk into their fun and creative lobby.

About ten minutes later a tall blonde came walking out of that room with a huge smile that just screamed, "I just nailed that interview, and you have a ridiculously tough act to follow... Good luck!"

Jeff, who by the way, had no idea of all that I had planned for this interview, immediately followed her. And, let's just say that he looked a little surprised by all of the junk that I had with me.

"Jeff, don't worry," I assured him through a cracking, dry throat. "I won't make a fool of you. Oh, and thanks for giving me that book to read."

He smiled, and again nodded. "No problem." A grin spread over his face from ear to ear. The last thing I remember him saying before I joined the huge assembly was, "Oh, crap! I've created a monster!"

As I rounded the corner into the room filled with the committee that was my interview, I gathered all of my courage and took the whole thing over -- recalling everything that I had just read in this precious book you are about to begin.

"Hi, everyone! My name is Jay and I am your 1:15 interview. I wanted to start off by giving you all a little gift to thank you for your time."

The first barnyard animal that I handed out was to David. Obviously, I was a little unsure as to how they were going to be received. I could have been kicked out of the town of Sumner at any minute for all I knew! But, by the time that I handed out the last one to Patti, I looked back over to David and he had already ripped his open like a kid on Christmas morning, and was holding that cows rear-end up to his mouth, devouring those jelly beans! I knew I was in the right place instantly! Everyone loved it!

Then, I passed around my photo album and explained why I brought it. Almost immediately, someone on the other side of the room was saying they had been to the very same obscure place as one that was pictured in that album. As the CD books went around, I heard Scott say, "I have this one. I've never met anyone else that has this."

The room was abuzz! Everyone was talking and asking questions. It was great! The interview continued. Sometimes it was as serious as most interviews are. Other times it was uproarious, and more fun than going out on a night on the town with a bunch of old friends. All of my nervousness was gone! I was feeling great!

Then it was time to play the banjo! I started to sweat. This was the first time that I had ever played in front of anyone! But, I remembered what this book taught me about these people, and myself for that matter. I decided to believe it, and they were for real!

I stood up and began to explain what I saw in my head when I wrote the song.

"Okay, I see really shaky animation, very simple drawings. It all starts with a freshly sprouted seedling blowing in the wind. It's having a hell of a time holding onto the soil. Then the scene flashes indoors, and there are about five little stick figures, smiling and working in a little room, packing coffee and loading trucks. The scene flashes back to that tree, and now its getting bigger and it's holding up to the wind a little better. Then back inside, there are about ten people working, laughing, and getting the job done. Now, back to that tree. It has roots and leaves now, and it even supports a nest on one of those limbs. Flash inside to even more people doing their jobs, still with smiles. Here goes…"

I started playing that banjo, only to flub the third note. I took a deep breath to gather myself and started again. This time it flowed like water! I closed my eyes and set my heart free. About halfway through the song I opened my eyes to survey the room. I couldn't believe what I saw. Everyone in that room had their eyes shut too! It was incredible. When I finished, everyone stood up and clapped!

The production was over. I said my goodbyes and left. I drove home feeling pretty proud of myself. I know what you're thinking. It sounds like a movie, right? I agree! It really was a moment for the silver screen, as far as I'm concerned.

What's better is the fact that I got the job. I'm not sure that I can express how it feels to be yourself completely in a job interview, and be rewarded for it. Two years later, Dillanos is everything, and more than I hoped it would be. My heart and career are really taking off like I could have never imagined.

What this book taught me is this: When there is a strong, clearly defined culture, whether it's in a city or a company, like minded people will flock to it and strengthen it, defend it and live it, almost giving it a life of its own. It builds a momentum that can't be stopped by any bump in the road.

Whether you use this book to better your business, to better yourself, or both, keep this quote from Dale Carnegie in mind, "The person who gets the farthest is generally the one who is willing to do and dare. The sure-thing boat never gets far from shore."

The Law of Opposites

Howard Heyer, Chairman of the Board

Often you get the best insights by pairing extremes with common objectives.
- C. Wright Mills

Formula 2:

Live by extremes in fun and discipline, with the power of personal ownership and empowerment bouncing off the walls.

Who would have thought the universal law of opposites would best sum up the essence of what creates the magic in our dynamic little company? It took me hours to zero in on the reason for our family company's skyrocketing growth from a used coffee cart and espresso machine my stepson manned in early 1992, to being one of the Northwest's largest micro roasters. Suddenly it hit me like a brick wall: My sons' opposite personalities and strengths.

Sure, you've heard that opposites attract in romance, but what about in business? The symmetry and power behind the law of opposites is inescapable. Birth and death, male and female, love and hate, night and day, yin and yang, right brain and left brain help govern our lives. But can the law apply to business as profoundly as it does

Heal the bottom line and your soul by making your employees' needs and growth opportunities your first priority every day.

17

End the concept of work. Celebrate the reality of daily adventures and games to win.

elsewhere in life?

Before jumping into an answer, I need to tell you that I don't practice all of the ancient words of wisdom I read. Take the timeless advice of exercising moderation in all things. Moderation in any aspect of business is a fast track to down and out. We don't do <u>anything</u> in moderation at Dillanos. The law of opposites bursts out of our roasting plant with blinding white light.

Does the universal law of opposites apply to business? In the chapters ahead, you will fill your heart and mind with examples of people, justifying a huge "Yes" to that question. The reason that Dillanos has a license to thrill everybody who walks through our doors is because my sons unite what may seem to be poles apart: Outrageous fun and high accountability.

With the challenges of the economy, most companies are saying, "Employee empowerment and happiness be damned." Their employees are working overtime with the only additional benefit being the chance to keep their jobs.

Many people, especially those nearing and at the top of the food chain, are so busy polishing their ego that they don't learn a thing. It's simple: Listen to your heart and your sense of right and wrong. I know, life isn't that black and white. The fact is, it is that black and white. There is a right thing to do and a wrong thing to do in every decision you make.

You have to make the paradigm shift in your mind that there is no such thing as work, just a series of new adventures you can dig into and make happen with your own hands.

Early in the company's history, we didn't have the balance we needed between fun and accountability. Fun too quickly turned to profit worries that are no fun at all. My stepson, David (fun),

If you don't run the company for profit, everybody loses.

CEO and Dillanos' co-founder, is all about passion. His right-brain strengths include finding and maintaining long-lasting customer relationships and creating an outrageously fun and nurturing company culture.

My left-brain son, Chris (accountability), President of Dillanos, is all about ever-improving efficiency systems, balanced financial analysis and honest management. David and the staff appreciate Chris because of his pure heart, honesty on all issues and uncanny ability to balance income and expenses.

Since the early days, staff and our customers have tagged the two brothers as the perfect blend of fun and accountability. I have met few company leaders that alone combine these extremes to reach a company's full potential.

I hate to pigeonhole anybody, especially my own sons. I do

everything I can to nurture all aspects of leadership in each of them. But I must admit, each son is extremely gifted on the opposite ends of the spectrum.

Why is it such perfect chemistry between such opposites?

Who better than the Chairman of the Board of Dillanos (as well as being their father) to dig deep enough into their magic talents to reveal some attributes others can model?

> # No matter the crisis, keep your sense of humor and a light-hearted spirit.

Let's start with Dillanos' CEO, since David was the real passion behind what birthed a company named after his son, Dillon.

You have to be born with a sense of wonder and contagious

> # Know the numbers at all times, but only track the ones you can control on a daily basis.

excitement about life. Everything with David is an adventure. Who doesn't want to go on an adventure every day they come to work?

David doesn't enter a room, he charges into every room and every activity, like a front line soldier staging for battle. Dramatic arm waving, palm rubbing and laughter regularly accompany the grin on his face and sparkle in his eyes. Yes, laughter in good times and bad is one of the golden tips in creating balance.

To heck with "you can't do this or that" around employees, fearing that sexual harassment might follow. No employee resents brotherly love. And employees at Dillanos are loved like family members. David has a lot to do with that love along with the passion, loyalty and the 110 percent effort given by every single member of our staff.

Consider where you work or used to work. It is pretty hard to be creative when layered management creates a class society made up of those people who count and those who don't. Sure, the mission statement says everybody is equal, but when did you last work in or manage a place that really lives that promise?

Someone's feelings get hurt and David is right in the offender's office talking through what happened and making sure feelings are immediately healed. It's the same whether it's the receptionist or a vice president.

David acts exactly the same with every customer, large accounts and small. At Dillanos, we don't have to <u>say</u> we care about our customers. They can feel it in their heart and soul every day with every contact by any of our staff members.

His creativity in helping our customers create individualized and powerful brands is nothing short of incredible. They love his enthusiasm and caring ways.

WE'RE ON A MISSION

David created our mission statement before we had secured our first customer.

Help People.
Make Friends.
Have Fun.

Perfect. That's exactly how David lives his life, so the employees have an easy model to follow.

Remember, don't just talk it. Live it every day.

Now onto Dillanos' President, Chris Heyer. With Chris's quiet style, you would, at first blush, have a hard time believing he and David are brothers who relate so perfectly.

In fact, in recent years the men's two extreme strengths are beginning to seamlessly merge. They are equally committed to growing a culture built on fun and accountability. They forged our company values together and, side-by-side, built a large customer base over the years.

Never stop setting higher and higher efficiency and performance standards.

Whether they are in the same meeting or not, the two come to the same conclusions and recommended actions, whether it is budget planning or employee appreciation award candidates.

The brothers are smart

enough to recognize and celebrate each other's special strengths. That is something unique, a chief executive officer and a president publicly and privately celebrating each other's strengths, rather than looking to undermine credibility for selfish reasons.

Chris is a serious student of the latest lean management efficiency systems that net maximum profits. He always says no to the status quo. His credo? Never stop improving. It can always be done smarter and faster with Chris. He remains fiscally conservative, always posing the devil's advocate position on any of David's passionate ideas.

Chris takes incredible pride in crafting an employee review process every three months that ensures the interviewer grows as much from the critique as the interviewee.

From the latest product and systems management to the most contemporary employee productivity techniques, Chris is continually setting his personal and staff performance standards higher and higher.

I think one of the big reasons the Dillanos' staff loves Chris's management style is because behind all his demands, he is a caring and highly sensitive man who watches over and protects everything and everyone.

I can hear you thinking, David and Chris sound like boy scouts. While they slip and slide at times in how I've just characterized them, they pretty much live up to how I just defined their extreme strengths. Besides, this world needs a lot more boy scouts at the top.

Take a quick glance of how just a handful of Dillanos side-by-side fun and accountability dynamics validates my premise that the best companies are built on the law of opposites:

Fun	Accountability
Everybody shares in the adventure and fun.	Lean Management: Disciplined and highly focused training and oversight to ensure minimum labor and capital expense with regularly measured and ever-improving efficiency.
Almost every small and large group meeting is full of outrageous fun.	Nobody arrives late or allows interruptions other than emergencies. A crystal clean intended outcome drives the short-list agenda.
Everybody, starting with management, is on much more than a first name basis, sharing their whole personality and lives seven days a week.	Highly structured performance reviews conducted without exception four times annually; probe employees to be candid in assessing how management is living up to the company mission and core values. Employees are also required to dig soul-deep as they share their own strengths and weaknesses in context to company values.

Dillanos' primary focus is on giving every employee a sense of ownership in the company they love.

The team works from a professionally crafted business plan, pinpointing strengths and weaknesses, as well as profiling the competition and strategically positioning the Dillanos' brand to carve out a unique industry niche. Dillanos is right on track with meeting its five-year sales and profit margin goals. At a time when most specialty coffee micro roasters are flat to growing sales upwards of eight percent a year, Dillanos' sales have increased an average of thirty percent a year since the company started in 1992.

I could go on with this extreme comparison, but hopefully I have sparked your imagination enough to begin your page-turning journey into the heart of what makes our amazing company tick.

Most companies are deep into the accountability side of management. You will find that the majority of this book is dedicated to giving dimension to the personal as well as company benefit of fully embracing the outrageous fun needed to help your spirits and profits soar.

What the Heck is RTM?

By David J. Morris, Chief Executive Officer

Time is really the only capital that any human being has, and the only thing he can't afford to lose.

- Thomas Edison

Formula 3:

Make the speed of accomplishment a game everybody wants to play.

My name is David J. Morris. I am a chronic procrastoholic.

There I said it! The first step in realizing you have a problem is to admit it.

I was an "I'll think about it tomorrow" kind of guy since grade school. If a job was to be done, don't look to David. While I never openly admitted it, I was always looking for any angle to avoid action -- of any kind.

So what the heck is RTM? RTM stands for <u>R</u>ight <u>T</u>his <u>M</u>inute. Right is for doing the <u>right</u> thing and This Minute means <u>now</u>!

So you're probably wondering, what in the world would a chronic procrastinator be doing as chief executive officer of a fast growing coffee company? Even worse, who am I to be writing about the power of RTM?

Instant gratification, usually a negative term, can be fun and productive. But it has to be used in the RTM way.

I am hoping the lesson will wake up a few other procrastoholics into discovering what I learned just five years ago. I know you can use this information to transform your company and your life.

> # Planning isn't a science, it is an imprecise art. Don't get bogged down waiting until everything is perfect. Believe me, it never will be.

Before getting into this helpful new twist on that tired old subject known as "Time Management 101," I need to point out that I'm not talking about shooting from the hip. Of course, we have all worked with people who rush to conclusions, then strike out without the right facts. That was me a couple of years ago. This can be extremely frustrating and unproductive.

Notice I said <u>the right facts</u>. And for most action, you don't have to spend all day debating or contemplating them.

I am not talking about analysis paralysis here. We all know that no action is an action in itself. Indecision can lead to the death of your culture <u>and</u> ultimately your company.

So just make sure you have the meaning correct and relevant facts before dashing for the door like a wild person.

I know that most of us want to get all the facts and consider all the possible outcomes before taking an action. So get the facts and ask yourself these four simple questions. It won't take more that a couple of minutes.

RTM Quick Questions:

- What are the relevant facts -- <u>not</u> all the facts?
- How does this action fit into our long-term plans?
- Will this take us closer to our company's goals?
- What resources do I have to make this happen?

When used in the right way, RTM powers your every step and action like you wouldn't believe without experiencing it yourself.

Move! Do something right now! Quit talking, reading and analyzing. It's time to be proactive and make it happen.

I can promise you this, if you start to live this way and take RTM action, the results will blow you away. Of course it's not a magic bullet -- there's no such thing -- but it's a company-changing addition. Go for it!

Reduce the time between conception and implementation. Your customers love it, and it's contagious to your staff.

Here's a powerful example of RTM at work:

In one of Dillanos' marketing meetings, we decided to contact a local television personality and invite him to our new state-of-the-art roasting plant. This particular station was featuring a weekly segment where the anchor would go to different communities trying out other people's jobs. One week he was a baker, the next he was a teacher, so we figured we would ask him to act as roast master, dressed in Dillanos' attire during three 90-second news features. It is important to recognize that this promotional opportunity did not come from a member of the marketing team, but from Cassie, our executive assistant, who was eager to share an idea. At Dillanos, everyone's opinion counts.

Now remember, the Pacific Northwest is coffee country, with specialty coffee roasters around every corner. Starbucks and a host of other major brands are a stone's throw from the television station. We had what many would consider to be a slim to none chance of getting a "Yes" to our request.

We all loved the idea and, just like everything else at Dillanos, we wanted it to happen just about as fast as the thought came to us. So our marketing director quickly pulled together some background information to drive to the television station to personally pitch the story, which in itself, demonstrated the power of RTM.

Meanwhile, I decided the way to make the offer irresistible was to create a customized label with the television personality's name and picture on the signature blend. You know, it never hurts to play to the anchor's ego a little. I enthusiastically "convinced" our very busy graphic artist, Paul, to take on an almost impossible task of developing a custom label. I knew, based on my own graphics experience, it could be done within

RTM can also be used for a quick turnaround from a bad decision.

an hour. So complete with a professional look, it was printed on glossy adhesive paper. We attached it to several one-pound bags and were ready to go.

Our marketing director was already en route to Seattle to make the pitch when I gave him a call.

"Lon, where are you?" I asked. "On my way to the television station," he said.

With a smile in my voice, I told him to turn around and come back. We wanted him to bring along the bags of beans with the custom label.

"That's impossible. Paul hasn't had the project more than an hour," he said. "There's design, printing…"

"Don't forget RTM, Lon. Hurry up and get back here. You won't believe this label!"

I bet you can guess how this story ended. Not only did the television anchor love the custom packaging, but also he was out at our roasting plant with his crew in less than a week.

The three-part series was posted in streaming video on www. dillanos.com within three weeks of the initial brainstorm.

Another example of RTM is something I like to call the "Bathroom Technique." Here is how it works. I am at a point in a meeting when there is a decision to make a phone call relevant to the topic at hand. Without interrupting the meeting, I quietly excuse myself for a moment "to go to the bathroom," and make that contact on my cell phone. In less than five minutes, I am able to return to the meeting with the response.

While you have to use good judgment when and when not to dash in and out of a meeting someone else is leading, more often than not, this technique will add to its value and outcome.

The national magazine *Selling Power* had heard about the Dillanos' way of making things happen in sales. A bold quote in a feature story on Dillanos Coffee Roasters says, "At specialty coffee trade shows, attendees are surprised to get back to their hotel rooms and find a follow-up email from a Dillanos' salesperson they met less than two hours before."

I guarantee you that nobody has more fun or gets new business from industry trade shows than Dillanos. We make a game out of contacting people the fastest. Our sales staff will have made three calls and be closing in on sealing a purchase agreement with a potential customer by the time the competition has fully profiled and considered whom to contact on their prospect list.

For many of our sales reps, a computer linked to the Internet has become their lifeblood. They hop on the prospect's website and profile them in a few minute's time before a planned meeting or minutes after the unexpected contact.

While nothing replaces face-to-face interaction, e-mail can begin forming a relationship you can build on.

I have to credit a big part of Dillanos' growth to the power of RTM in sales. Quick response in every aspect of sales gives us a unique edge and instant evidence to customer prospects that they can count on us to take care of their needs now!

We have our salespeople check their emails via laptop every hour. If customers would like to meet, our salespeople can email their reply with a copy of their daily Palm Pilot calendar, leaving it up the customer to fill in a time slot that works for them.

I could fill this entire book with examples of our staff living the power of RTM, but you get the idea.

Remember though, RTM isn't always the answer. Annual budget planning, capital investments, acquisitions, employee performance reviews and a short list of other activities benefit from patiently investing time to ensure a quality outcome.

Notice, I said short list.

Chasing after and getting new customers, saving those about to leave and just about every other daily action can and should be turned into an adventure in making big things happen in little time.

I would rather see our staff enthusiastically grab onto what they perceive to be the right facts, then aborting if it turns out to be the wrong direction, versus losing an opportunity over indecision and inaction. At least they are doing something, and with guidance and experience, they'll hit the nail on the head nine times out of ten.

I bet you didn't know that airplanes fly off exact course over ninety percent of the time. That's right. Only a small percentage of the time is the plane exactly on course. If a pilot really worried about being exact, they would never leave the ground.

Too often we regret having taken the wrong action when the problem can be corrected in minutes, just by using RTM. Big deal, you made the wrong decision. Buck up and head in the right direction.

Leave your ego at the door and decide to undo the damage as quickly as you helped create it. How many of us have spent minutes coming up with an idea and then defend it for hours, regardless of its merits.

Grab onto the power of RTM and soon you will fi nd those around you either jump on board or are soon left behind. Since our humble beginnings, one of the things that has differentiated Dillanos from the other companies in our industry is our culture of acting on every assignment as though it is a grand adventure, a game of beat-the-clock that none of us would live without.

Remember, if saying "I'm not sure" is death, then saying, "Let's hold off" is suicide. Follow the plan -- then do it "Right This Minute."

Be Like Abe

By Chris Heyer, President

Honesty isn't a policy at all; it's a state of mind or it isn't honesty.

- Eugene L'Hote

Formula 4:

Be honest in all things, even when no one is looking.

It's all about doing the right thing.

The foundation of ethics is the simple concept of trying to be honest with yourself and everyone else. That means not rationalizing or using all too-familiar language like this:

- "Our financials have a fudge factor of ten percent."
- "Everyone rounds up their numbers when they talk to the media."
- "He manipulated the truth during parts of his testimony."
- "Oh, he always embellishes the truth when he retells the story."
- "It was just a little white lie."
- "I stretched the truth a bit."
- "He didn't ask, so I didn't tell him the whole story. It isn't like I lied or anything."
- "I blurred the lines a bit."
- "Everyone does it."

Admit it. We have all done. If asked, my hand is the first to go up.

If there is one thing we are all good at, it is finding language that softens the fact that we lied about something. If we were all to hold ourselves to the dictionary's definition of truth, we would never deviate an inch from "<u>total conformity with known facts.</u>"

You can't build a creative and personally fulfilling culture if it isn't grounded in absolute honesty.

Now don't get me wrong. Nobody is perfect. What I am talking about here is creating a culture where everybody in the company asks, "Is this the right thing to do?" as part of their decision-making process. If the answer is "No," then under no circumstances is that action to be taken, regardless of perceived financial gain.

Of our six company values, number one is, "Have honesty, integrity and professionalism in everything we do." This is not just a phrase on the wall; it is lived every day, starting with top leadership.

If your company is like most in North America, you already have the typical goals posted everywhere to "inspire" staff.

Be ready to listen to and act on employee feedback.

Let's focus on the benefits of trying to be honest before I get into some simple ways to get there.

If you don't have clear, simply stated core values to accompany your mission, write them right now.

The problem is that the "top" people who went on that weekend retreat to write the mission statement and goals are almost always the very people who violate them every day. You need to create an open and honest culture where subordinates are able to call the boss on not doing the right thing.

At Dillanos, everybody from our bookkeeper to packagers, have free license to call management and the overall company on not living our mission and core values. We encourage performance reviews that urge brutally candid feedback on our daily culture.

The benefit of getting honest with yourself and each other on the job is that Dillanos has an unbelievably low turnover rate. When there is a problem in employee relations, it

No client or meeting should interrupt the need for immediacy in resolving employee conflicts.

almost always gets down to telling the truth.

In our company, the minute a personal issue comes up, we put the two people together to "get honest" and work out the issues and differences <u>right now</u>. The result is virtually no game playing and bad mouthing that eats up huge amounts of potentially productive time in competing companies.

The same principle applies when it comes to snide remarks about the competition or suppliers. Management should never disparage the competition. Your company is the only competition. Constant self-improvement is what great companies are all about.

Even not-so-ethical decisions made behind

Honesty must be lived without compromise behind closed doors to be credible in the rest of the building.

close doors will eventually filter down and permeate the culture. The reason for this is simple. Let's say you have not been honest with a customer. To make it so they don't find out, you'd have to tell everyone within your company that has contact with that customer. Imagine the message that sends to your employees. Or, if you don't tell anyone, you put your employee in a compromising position.

I must admit, telling the absolute truth to customers isn't

always comfortable. For example, one time a potential customer asked one of our sales reps about the viability of a particular drive-thru location for a coffee business. Keith, our sales manager at the time, told him that based on the difficulty getting in and out of the driveway, he didn't think the investment was worth the risk. The potential customer was offended at his honesty and decided to use another company as his coffee supplier. He opened his location and sure enough, it was mediocre at best.

So you are asking yourself what good came out of being so honest?

Well, just imagine what would have happened if you would have stroked his ego, just to get the account. He would have come back and said, "Why didn't you tell me? I trusted you. You guys are the experts."

> It takes years to build a culture based on honesty, and only seconds to lose it.

We will always benefit in the long term because word quickly gets around that we are genuinely interested in our customers' success. This serves as the foundation for all we do as their roaster and business partner. It is important to point out that within a half mile, on the other side of the road, there are now two high-volume locations that use our coffee.

If you find yourself squirming or a thought just flashed through your mind of a recent "shading" of the truth or an outright lie, you know what has to be done to begin creating a creative culture.

We are not talking about the big stuff here. If you are considering insurance fraud or tax evasion, you need to read another book. We are talking about the little decisions you make every day that can easily be rationalized.

Another way to turn that, though, is that if your company does what other companies do when it comes to absolute honesty, how can you expect to create a uniquely dynamic culture?

As a company, we truly believe in the old sayings, "What goes around, comes around," and "You reap what you sow."

Dillanos is distinguishing itself as a fast growing, highly profitable company by keeping it simple and honest. Be honest in all things, even when no one is looking.

We Don't Need No Education

By Scott Hinckley, Vice President

I have never let my schooling interfere with my education.

- Mark Twain

Formula 5:

While education can be important, potential fit within your culture is what matters most.

Simply put, education and past experience is not always an accurate measurement of the value or potential productivity of the individual.

To us, cultural understanding and fit is the single most important asset in terms of personal success and productivity.

Whether interviewing a potential new employee or talking with a seasoned veteran, your number one job is to make sure they know, understand and live your company's mission and values.

Without focusing first on a person's comfortable fit within the culture, you are limiting employee potential.

Empowering those who don't share the common thread of your culture can be your largest problem in terms of productivity. Despite their own personal abilities or hard work, their true value may not pan out when you analyze the big picture. This happens because their attitude or feeling of purpose is usually the first thing to go. They tend to retreat from being part of the group and often only keep to their personal agenda. This shelters them from the positive nature of the group and further reduces their exposure to the culture.

Employee productivity and growth potential is reduced with the absence of enthusiasm. All the traditional management prodding in the world can't fix this problem.

The first big mistake you can make is confusing hard work for productivity. I have seen one person in a management role single-handedly destroy the morale of an entire production staff. I bet you have too.

This guy was fast, really fast and worked harder than most. The problem was that he hated every second of his assigned duties. His first issue was that he constantly compared his actions to the actions of others and disregarded the values of our culture.

While others grouped together to organize and plan for growth, this manager felt there was no time to think or plan, only to work. His unwillingness to spend the time creating and improving systems only compounded his workload as business increased. He soon developed an obvious bitterness toward the company and much of the

Don't confuse hard work and ability with productivity and potential.

staff because he felt he had no support. His employees were troubled by his opinion that they didn't work hard enough. He truly felt that if he wasn't enjoying work, they shouldn't either.

Instead of inspiring through the inherent enthusiasm of creating efficiency that is built into our culture, he opted for spreading his negative attitude throughout the entire production line and brought productivity to a halt.

While other departments were having fun and taking part in company events that added to their fulfillment, he was performing tasks that people would no longer willingly do because he had lost all influence. This was a manager who felt that carrying the weight of the entire department made him worth more to the company.

The lonely path that he chose to take was the expressway to burnout, and burn out he did.

> Whether in an initial interview or talking to long-term employees, clearly and continually communicate what is expected in terms of cultural understanding and involvement.

HELP PEOPLE

An employee who can truly trust the culture will be more open to confidently bring heartfelt honesty to management.

When he realized that he wasn't capable of being fulfilled with his work, he abruptly left the company.

I learned a great deal from working with his staff. Simply put, he just didn't see the big picture. He saw the growth of the company as a hindrance that just created more work. Most importantly, he did nothing toward involving his staff in making the department more efficient as a whole. His answer was always to work harder. He was quick, he was skilled and did more work than the average Joe, but his potential was limited. The result of his poor attitude and lack of cultural buy-in meant low productivity by his entire department.

A look from afar showed a quick, productive "set the pace by example" leader. A closer look at the big picture revealed that he not only lowered his own potential with his attitude, but also the potential of his department staff.

Help People, Make Friends and Have Fun. It's easy to remember a mission statement that holds our staff accountable to three simple human wants.

Our personal conduct and coffee-related core values statement digs deeper into the mission statement, providing a clear road map of highly expected behavior standards at Dillanos.

Those who refuse to Help People, Make Friends and Have Fun just don't stick around. Those who measure their actions to the culture tend to commit to a growing career at Dillanos.

> Good or bad employee performances always tie actions to values, to mission, and to culture.

Imagine a company full of employees that have the same want and vision as the founders had the day they started the company.

This is the same drive that has powered small firms into worldwide enterprises. Does Starbucks come to mind?

> Trust comes from management's ability to actively and respectively listen to each staff member.

Believe me, Dillanos makes "bad" hires too. Some people first profess to love our highly defined culture, until they start living it. They have spent a lifetime comfortably

Never set people up for failure. Use drive to set and reach achievable goals.

blaming the companies they've worked for, not acting as a contributing architect to constant improvement.

The best answer Dillanos has found to keeping "bad" hires low is quickly spotting those who really spark as they learn about our culture. All eyes are searching for that sense of genuine understanding and enthusiasm during multiple interviews with several department heads.

Every interviewer asks questions we can directly relate to our culture to see if there are any pre-existing values that conflict with ours. If it is evident that there is not a commitment to top-of-the-line customer service or an understanding of the importance of efficiency, the interview process is cut short.

Negotiate goals and deadlines with your employees.

We start every review with the same question, "How do you feel Dillanos is living up to its mission?" That is followed by, "What about you, how do you feel you live up to the mission?" If the answers don't seem confident, then it's one of two things; they don't trust you or they don't understand well enough to trust the culture.

If an employee can look at his manager and explain a specific example of when the company acted outside of its values, that employee has trust in you and the company and feels an ownership that transcends the boss / employee relationship.

We list our core values on the front page of our review form and ask that each employee select a value that encompasses them the most. We also ask which value seems to be the hardest to reach. Any answer you get paints a picture of their understanding of what those values mean to them on the job. Now both of you have a common point of measurement. One of the most important things you can do is become an active listener. Let employees do the talking.

I had some difficulties early on in my management career with Phil when he was Dillanos' Roasting Manager. He was having a challenging time defining the worth of his role in his own mind, which resulted in an emotional roller coaster. Although we were all continually amazed by his abilities to roast and taste coffee, he still wasn't fulfilled. Phil felt like he had reached a dead end in his career.

I regularly questioned Phil about what he wanted. "Tell me what you are really after," I would ask. He began to bombard me with ideas about his potential role in marketing and sales as the definitive voice of the quality of our product. You could see it in his eyes and he assumed that role right in front of me. It turned out that Phil wanted to be more of a celebrity personality within the company. He was beginning to articulate a perfect role for a micro roasting company's roast master.

Phil needed staff and customers to see him as even more than just another coffee roaster. He puts his soul into his work and he desperately wanted to teach and share his passion for his work with our customers and the North American coffee industry.

With trust, you are handed the ability to motivate and create an environment where success reigns supreme.

Phil had little experience walking the ranks of the industry and even less experience as a public speaker. What Phil did possess was an above average commitment to our culture. He would stop at nothing to consistently exceed customers' roast expectations.

Throughout my own life, I have weighed myself down with a lack of self-confidence and a fear of social interaction. I always considered that success was a big paycheck, a prestigious award or degree, all of which seemed out of reach for me. I never saw myself as a leader and certainly never thought I would be the vice president of such an amazing company.

I worked on computers, fixed coffee roasters or streamlined warehouse production efficiency. The only move up for me was management. I had developed skills and knowledge within our industry, but possessed zero experience in managing others. I had absolutely no confidence as a leader.

Why on earth would anybody put me in charge? I had failed in two separate industries and never finished college. I would not be perceived as the most outstanding candidate for a leadership position.

The guidance and leadership of Dillanos' President, Chris Heyer, and CEO, David Morris, proved to me my value as a person, an employee and eventually a manager.

"It's great having you around. Everyone loves working with you," David would say often enough that it started to resonate down to my soul. That confidence in my potential started me on the path of accomplish-ment.

For the first time in my life, I felt genuinely appreciated. I could finally say I love my job.

Why me? Management sensed my one hundred percent commitment to our highly defined culture. Much to my surprise, that in itself was enough for them to place their bets and offer me a position in management.

Chris and David knew that if I could live the mission and be true to the culture, people would trust and follow, just as I had trusted and followed them.

True leaders share in the success and failures of their team.

Obstacles are always going to be different and, at times, hard to admit. Sometimes you have to reveal a type of honesty that you usually reserve for family.

I wouldn't be here today if it wasn't for one of Dillanos' staff members who candidly pinpointed my own faults. Opportunity to survive, then grow in the company was within easy grasp. I just had to ease up on my ego to see my problems and correct them.

I was given the time, thoughtful consideration and constructive input I needed to set personal goals and deadlines.

Speaking of goals and deadlines, management always negotiates with each employee to get their sincere ownership.

It all boils down to trust. If an employee trusts you and knows that your actions are based upon the values of your culture, they will often set goals and deadlines that exceed your expectations.

Cheers!

By Keith Hayward, Vice President Sales & Marketing

Appreciation is a wonderful thing. It makes what is excellent in others belong to us as well.

- Voltaire (known to have consumed more than 50 cups of coffee per day)

Formula 6:

Celebrate each other's successes.

Cheers! This statement means a lot in itself: to gladden, celebrate, encourage, shout with applause, to hearten, uplift. These descriptions are powerful and energetic. They tell a story and create a setting that looks like the place and people where I spend most of my time.

I have the privilege to live in and experience a company culture where we repeat these descriptions like a mantra. They are spoken every time we grab that glorious moment to recognize and share in each other's successes. Work without success or the ability to recognize co-workers' triumphs is just what it sounds like. Work.

But a place that believes in every employee's importance, appreciates their input and dedication, shares in their accountability and relishes in their success is a place we call Dillanos.

It was an eye-opening experience when I first walked into Dillanos. My first memory reflects on my job interview with David, Chris and Howard sitting around a small conference table. The atmosphere of the building and meeting room had a clubhouse or break room atmosphere, rather than the traditional stodgy conference room feeling.

David was excitable, anxious to tell a story and everyone

was laughing. I couldn't help but smile; any feelings of anxiety or discomfort were instantly gone. The interview was different than any I'd had before. They described a company they had created based on values, friendships and a mutual desire to share and win. Together. The interview seemed to focus more on how I could fit in with these ideals rather than my past work experience. They were so infectious, so happy and proud of their unique corporate culture. I was immediately hooked, finding myself thinking, "Is this real?"

> Make sure your prospective employees get a sense of your company's culture right from the start.

Even on the chance that it was real, I wanted to see for myself. Simply put, I remember thinking that I just wanted to be around these guys and that positive energy. I accepted the job immediately.

I knew things were going to be pretty interesting from the start. I had a challenging and somewhat daunting task ahead of me. I was actually hired to replace David as the lead salesperson. The footsteps I was hired to follow were indeed large and filled with a passion for quality and commitment that could only be filled by an owner. Or so I thought.

Encouraged by my ambition and, at the same time, patient

with my youth and limited knowledge of the industry, we created a unique focus. My efforts leaned toward selling the idea of the company, the friendships and relationships that we were trying to create.

Imagine walking into a position where you were expected to portray the passion and pride of the owners into a product you were just getting to know. Well, my task was not as difficult as I had expected. Even in the first few weeks, spending time with David and Chris opened my eyes. The contagious feeling of pride and belief in each other easily carried me through that learning process.

Starting with limited product knowledge and inflated expectations, my early failures became eye-opening learning experiences. I noticed that these failures were experienced and felt not just by me, but also by David. The reason I succeeded is simple. I was welcomed as one of them, part of the family.

We got upset and learned together or we cheered and celebrated together. I remember David patiently walking me through my first sale,

Make sure new employees understand the "big picture" of your company's operation, not just their duties.

step-by-step, just to reward me joyously when the deal closed. He praised me for a success that, when I look back now, I know I wouldn't have been able to complete without him. That very real excitement and praise was my baptism into a company boasting a unique culture. That culture was created based on the fact that as the company grew we could <u>all</u> celebrate "our" successes!

We are never afraid to give credit for the victories and successes that we share. We win as a team and we lose as a team. Ours is a shared responsibility.

Every member of our team is essential and understanding that is one of the greatest strengths a leader can possess. This is a trait embraced by our company's leadership and passed down through example. No one stands alone.

It's reminiscent of the Academy Awards, when the winning actor steps forward to receive the Oscar. They usually end up naming the whole cast and crew, wanting to share the honor and spotlight with them. This selfless affection and respect for co-workers creates friendships and relationships that are more commonly associated with a social organization than a business.

Dillanos handles new employee orientation different than many other companies. You will not find the hurried "here's your desk and job" attitude that seems prominent in today's workplace. Instead, each new employee works in every department in the company during their introductory phase. Regardless of their job assignment, they all learn the ins and outs of the company before starting their job.

There are a few reasons for this:

1. You really get to know each person and get a good insight into his or her responsibilities.
2. New hires learn how the departments interact with each other.
3. Working in each other's departments lets you really see and experience what that department constitutes as a success.

Then, you are able to recognize those successes in the future!

A fair-weather management style of leadership would be unwelcome and short-lived in our company! There are no finger-pointers here, no blamers and no discipline with shared responsibility. We live under the premise that you are only as strong as your weakest link. For that reason, we surround that link with the strength, support and opportunity to grow stronger every day.

The opportunity to learn is relished. We grow with every lesson and mistakes are seldom repeated.

When those who carried you through your success give you the first credit and kudos of winning, it is incredible! It is an unselfish sharing of energy and triumph, similar to the experience felt at a church revival or listening to a dynamic motivational speaker.

Competition in our industry is plentiful. Our competitors are talented -- and hungry. We stand ahead of the pack because we are ridiculously sincere, squeaky clean and thrive on sharing in each of the company's successes. Pride takes a back seat to responsibility because responsibility to the company and each other is what really breeds success.

How many bosses or leaders will critique your performance, speech or training session and then ask you to critique theirs? Learning together and constantly challenging each

How you bring a customer in the door is more important than just the financial reward of the new client's income stream.

other breeds personal and professional growth. It also creates a support system of accountability.

Success is more attainable when the destination is clear to everyone. It is much more rewarding when everyone has a part. On the rare times that we fail, it is easier for all of us as a team to focus in on the target and dissect what went wrong. There are times when we find some elements totally out of our control – but we learn from the experience. Some outsiders believe that it is a big and cumbersome process to involve so many people on so many levels. Based on our corporate culture, we find that sharing in each other's successes and failures is a true sign of mutual respect, admiration and growth.

It has been useful to look at other companies' case history

successes. We have found they can be useful tools in understanding why they handled a situation in a certain way. We look at those successes and then create our own rules.

Believe it or not, our sales force is not cutthroat with each other! They truly help one another. Our sales areas overlap because we believe that the right fit is a crucial ingredient in keeping customers. Teamwork is our real strength. Self-serving braggarts don't fit in. We want to succeed with like-minded partners. It requires searching to find the right staff members. Those individuals realize success is just as much about teamwork and character as it is about performance.

The definition of success in a sales position is cut and dry. If you close sales, bring in business, show the boss the money, then you are successful. Right? Wrong! The financial element is what every company needs to survive. But how you bring in that money is just as important. Success isn't just a dollar sign.

We are firm believers that success is shared with our customers. Knowing our customers on a more intimate level helps us to recognize their success as well. To have a successful business, both the company and its customers have to succeed together. By strengthening our value to our customers through a partnership, it becomes a win-win situation. They have no desire to look somewhere else.

It feels great to call one of our customers and recognize them for opening a new franchise location or congratulate them on their first year anniversary. Congratulating them on the quality of their employees is also participating with that customer in their success!

We know we have succeeded in that relationship when our customers call to give us unsolicited rave reviews about our product, services and most importantly, our employees.

 7

All in the Family

By Paul Balmer, Art and Media Director

A true family grows and moves through life together, inseparable in the heart.
- Doc Childre and Howard Martin

Formula 7:

I know what you're thinking. This is work! What's family got to do with it? Or perhaps, you are starting to get the horrible feeling that this is going to be a "let's all get together, bang on some drums and tell each other how much we love one another" chapter.

Well, you're right.

I'll give you a second to grab your drum. Just kidding. But before you jump on over to the next chapter, let's talk about the enormous, no, gargantuan, no, colossal effect treating company employees as family will have on your enterprise's future.

Have I peaked your interest? Great! Let's do this.

As humans we all have a need to belong. Make sure everyone feels like they belong in your company's family.

Lyndon Baines Johnson once said, "The family is the cornerstone of our society. More than any other force it shapes the attitude, the hopes, the ambitions and the values of the child. And when the family collapses it is the child who is usually 'damaged.'" What if we substituted the word "child" with the word "company"? Whoa. Heavy stuff, but do you see where we're going with this?

Your company will thrive in a family atmosphere. I know because I'm part of the Dillanos' family. Now I've worked at companies that were the antithesis of Dillanos.

They were profitable, but since working at Dillanos I see just how much more fulfilling and profitable these companies could have been at no extra expense.

Successful companies are all about family, not the bottom line.

Imagine. In the right company culture, you don't have to deal with that sinking feeling on Sunday nights, just knowing you have to get up in the morning and "do it all over again."

The great thing about our leadership is they know that by becoming successful and reaching our goals they are endangering the very reason they became successful. When a company grows, just the mere fact of getting bigger starts to eat away at the foundation of the camaraderie and spirit that it took to create the venture in the first place.

By realizing that being a family is one of the magical pieces to this elusive puzzle of success, we can now emphasize and focus on it daily. I'm not talking about a bunch of insincerity here either.

We honestly try to create this unique culture through our actions, making life easier for those around us even if it takes a little extra effort on our part.

First of all, what does family mean to you?

What does it mean to the people where you work? Everybody has a different story when it comes to family. Some great; some not so great. Since everyone has a slightly different idea of what family is, create a family-like culture that is unique to your organization; one that everyone identifies with and relates to in the same, positive way.

Here's the catch. It all starts with me -- and you! You have got to make it happen! This is where we realize that it's not all about the bottom line. In fact, your bottom line relies on your "family"

Make "big" meetings full of fun and memorable small moments.

thinking you don't just care about the bottom line. Life is so much more than that.

I've worked in some positions, not so far from the bottom of the organizational chart, where the leaders actually thought they were doing all the right things. But you could smell their insincerity from a mile away. Needless to say there wasn't a family environment in any of those places.

So how do we make our business a family business? It would be downright weird if we just walked in the door one day and started giving everyone bear hugs. Well, you don't have to get too radical, just structure a simple plan and go for it. A good way to do this is have a great mission statement.

When Dillanos' mission statement was created, it was formulated with customers, as well as employees in mind to help ensure a family environment. We all naturally want to help those close to us and certainly everyone wants to have fun. Did the kids in school that never seemed to fit in seem to be having very much fun? Heck no. If you don't feel like

> # Respect one another, and take joy in all aspects of each other's lives.

part of the group, you aren't going to feel free to cut loose, burst with creativity and have some fun. Our casual and simple mission statement sets the tone for our highly personal company style.

When employees start looking at things from the "family" point of view, it becomes contagious. People start to view customers as extended family and go way beyond the extra mile to make these new family members feel like just that, family members.

Starting to sound hokey yet?

Just ask our competitors how effective we are at winning over their customers.

Trust me, we don't bad mouth anybody. Ever. But if our sales staff is given half a chance to introduce somebody to our culture by taking a plant tour, consider the business ours the majority of the time.

Okay, before you start to think that everyone here at Dillanos Coffee Roasters has had one too many double lattes and this whole family thing is too good to be true, let's get real for a minute. Of course we have issues. It's a business, after all. But our employees are encouraged to tell it like it is on a daily basis to top management and managers, whether it is good or bad.

Bad or hurt feelings don't stagnate around here. If something isn't out in the open, department heads bolt into action to get to the bottom of the issue Right This Minute.

It's funny how much effort we will put into something when we want and love to do it, as opposed to how little we are willing to invest when we are forced into something. One good way of getting people to identify with the family business culture is by openly praising those who are already on board, believe in it and are living that way.

Personally, I think the very best way to make your family business paradigm take affect is to make it contagious from the top down. I've witnessed David, our CEO, not just pat people on the back or give out hand-throbbing high fives, but actually do cartwheels across the floor when somebody has done something extraordinary! Well, they were sort of cartwheels . . .

Who doesn't want to see the boss get a little crazy with pride and enthusiasm sometimes? We love it! And of course, we all join in on the fun.

Years ago in basic training, my platoon experienced a rare thing. Our drill sergeants treated us fairly and with respect. This doesn't mean they didn't expect the world and more from us. It just meant that when we gave them what was needed, we were recognized for it.

The standard is that drill sergeants tear down and torture their recruits whether they do good or bad.

When our platoon scored highest on a test in our company or set a course record, we were rewarded with time off and a rousing game of rugby.

You can probably guess which platoon scored the highest possible scores on every test, course or skill we came across. Another amazing thing happened as well. We started to feel like a family, drill sergeants included.

In our last company roll call before graduation, my friend and I felt it might be appropriate for our platoon to stand in formation with corncob pipes in our mouths. I look back now and wonder what we were thinking. In our youthful bliss, we purchased pipes for everyone in our platoon, plus a couple of extras. As we came to attention, every one of us put a pipe in our mouth.

Amazingly, my drill sergeant knew exactly who had instigated the whole thing and promptly confronted me, nose to nose. He yelled, "Men, we are a family and in my platoon that means we will all stand as one in uniform! Balmer! I suggest you provide me with the proper uniform!" With that said, I hesitantly pulled the extra pipes from my pocket and handed them to him. I can tell you honestly it was the proudest moment in my military career to see our two drill sergeants, standing in the bitter Kentucky cold, with the last two corncob pipes sticking out of their mouths.

I don't know if they ever caught any flack. They never told us, but I do know every single one of us would have followed them to hell and back that day. We were family.

Lead by example.
Be excited.
Be open.
Be sensitive.

Get to know your family. What makes them tick? What's going on in their lives? Be understanding through their ups and downs. Dare I even pull out the "L" word here? Break out the drums people. I'm goin' for it. Yes, you guessed it. Love everybody! Can you have a family environment without it? That's the secret to being sincere with everyone. When they know you care, for real, then you're getting somewhere.

I've known the leaders at Dillanos since before Dillanos was even a thought. David and I went to school together. They all possess a natural love for everyone that goes well beyond the norm. So, of course, Dillanos just evolved into a family environment. The challenge is to keep it that way as the company grows. Judging by the fact that every single employee loves Dillanos, I'd say we're on

MAKE
FRIENDS

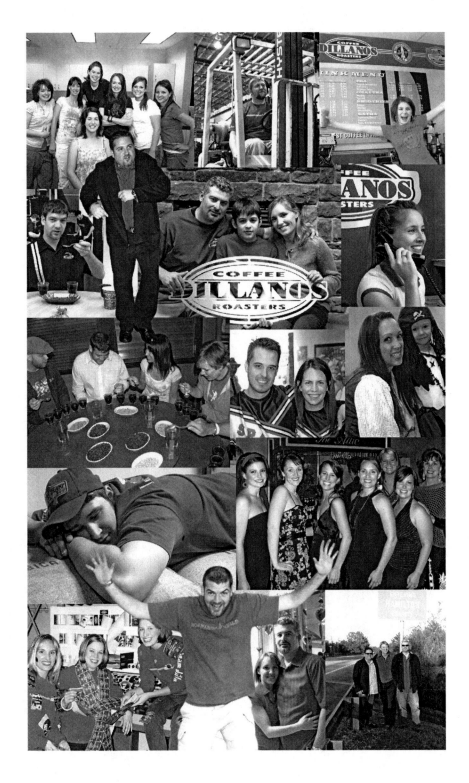

the right track.

Remember, a family that works together can accomplish anything!

Create a Sense of Eternal Youth, Energy and Excitement

By Lon LaFlamme, Marketing Director

The precious spirit of youth lies solely in the heart.

- John Boyle O'Reilly

Formula 8:

**Keep the curiosity, wonder and freshness
of youth alive in everybody.**

I scanned my memory files on Dillanos to determine where I might be able to give the reader a special takeaway. In no time, I realized that one of the distinguishing factors at Dillanos is the median age of employees: twenty-eight.

Only one employee besides Chairman of the Board, Howard Heyer, is over fifty, and that is me. I'm a ripe old age of fifty-four.

Be generous with your real smile and caring nature.

In my brief tenure at Dillanos, I have learned how to navigate as a fifty-something-year-young contributor.

For you handful of hardy souls who are over the age of forty, you know that fitting into the youth scene can be hard and, at worst, embarrassing.

So what happened to me in a little less than a year that makes me feel no different in age than any of Dillanos' employees?

Why do I feel younger in spirit and step than I have for twenty years?

What is the secret behind this magic fountain of youth I drink

78

from every day at the office?

Pardon the pun, but have I perked your interest yet? Who doesn't want to wake up every day feeling the curiosity, wonder, optimism and bright-eyed innocence of youth?

Before I step forward into the mystery and answers to these engaging questions, I need to take a few steps back, back into my classic past in corporate America.

As I mentioned in the foreword of this book, I have been schooled in business up to my eyeballs, receiving all the right diplomas and special management schooling to run the $100+ million company I led for many years.

If you ever read Gail Sheehy's 1980s runaway best-seller titled *Passages*, you know the guideposts of my life story.

I got married at twenty-one, just after finishing my bachelor's degree in journalism. I bought a new washer and dryer -- my first -- then a house. By the time I was thirty-five I had three kids, a job in the corner office and a divorce.

If you think your company is cutthroat, try the advertising business. I think Neil Simon pretty well nailed it in his Broadway play and movie, *Prisoner on Second Avenue*. It is

Don't just accept change, constantly instigate it.

a battle of smiles, wiles and strategy, as every able soul battles to make it to vice president and a window office.

Those daring few who really bite off yesteryear's definition

Everybody needs to be computer literate, utilizing the latest technological advances in personal and organizational management.

of the American Dream ruthlessly pursue the biggest palatial reward of all, chief executive officer. At Fortune 500 companies, the position comes with too many perks and privileges to list.

The American Dream: Power, money, great vacations, a house bigger than you could ever really need. Most importantly, society's blessing that you have arrived.

Sound great?

Take it from someone who scaled those cliffs and lavishly bathed in the purported material rewards. It really can be lonely at the top. That's just the tip of the iceberg when it comes to the old top-down management world that raised an opportunist like me.

Sound like a happy ending? Now for that typical corporate America dose of reality.

After nearly twenty-five years growing up in the same traditional dog-eat-dog company, I decided I had had enough of the American Dream.

I was mad, cynical, suspicious and old in soul years.

I had made enough to sell my stock, retire to teach marketing at the nation's largest private university and write the great American novel.

Through the writing of literally thousands of pages, feeling every emotion of being young, old, a child, an adult, a rebirth of freshness and hope began to emerge. My corporate-weary soul was healing.

While serving as an adjunct professor, a youthful optimism began flowing through my veins again. I couldn't imagine returning to a traditional job. Those alternative lifestyles I had dismissed as a rationale for losers for years was suddenly coming into focus.

There was a better way to live, a self-directed way.

With the stock market plunge, so went my profit cushion. I finally had to trudge back down to the dark and dirty mine fields of business for a few years.

After a number of promising Madison Avenue interviews and consideration as marketing director of major national retail brands, I found myself withdrawing from the marketplace even further. I just couldn't return to a "traditional" job, a "traditional" company.

I decided to limit the amount of money I would make and maximize on a self-directed business lifestyle. Like so many young people today, it took me too many years to learn the true definition of success. I didn't have a clue how to separate a rich personal life from my five days a week on the job.

My first step was to write a new chapter in my business life by charting my own course as an independent marketing consultant.

My second big step in entering the job market with the spirit of youth, was charging into this technology-driven age with the twenty-something's commitment to understanding and using the latest technology.

Don't take yourself too seriously. Laugh at your weaknesses while correcting them.

I put together a modest website and sent out a handful of brochures, highlighting my extensive expertise in five industries.

Dillanos Coffee Roasters picked up on my senior specialty coffee experience and retained me to craft a strategic growth plan.

As I began researching the company's history and strengths and weaknesses, I was immediately set back by a sense of youthful energy and purpose every employee showed during probing interviews.

How could anybody really "love" a job, especially someone who didn't own it? Without exception, every employee spoke about what they contributed to the company with an owner's pride.

Loyalty is an understatement. While all salaries are modest; every single employee was filled with cornball enthusiasm, loyalty and passion for their precious company. Many had left higher paying jobs to join up with the Dillanos' gang for the adventure of their lives.

At the time of this writing, it has been just two quick years and everything about my business and many of the things in my personal life have made a quantum leap into Dillanos' warm glow.

9

Is Yesterday Soon Enough?

By Scott Wittmire, Shipping Manager and
John Berg, Head Delivery Driver

Service…
Giving what you don't have to give.
Giving when you don't need to give.
Giving because you want to give.
-Damien Hess

Formula 9:

Make an over-the-top commitment to customers.

<u>Scott Wittmire: Giving Everything</u>

Something profound happened in my life recently. My wife, Michelle, gave birth to our second child – a beautiful baby girl named Savannah Grace. As I held her for the first time, I knew that if I gave her anything less than everything, it just wouldn't be enough.

I still have the same feeling for my son, Ryan, born four years earlier and for our other children, Brandon, Kayla and Jesse, whom I have raised for most of their lives. Yes, the love that a father has for his family is unmatched.

Every day I feel a great responsibility and an unquenchable desire to give my family everything they need – sometimes before they are even aware they

> The commitment you make to your company, co-workers, customers and humanity should be no less than that made to your own family.

Nothing is impossible when a company acts as one unit, with everyone sharing the same heart and vision.

need it. From my perspective and experience, that's what lies at the foundation of a good family.

About two years ago, a different kind of life-changing event occurred for me.

Searching for secular fulfillment, I discovered a unique company with an idealistic outlook and youthful exuberance. This was apparent from the moment I stepped through the door for my first interview.

It is with great pride that I now say that I have a hand in keeping that youth and idealism alive as a member of the Dillanos Coffee Roasters family. I say "family" because that's the only word that can truly describe what we have.

Our culture, our principles and even our mission that drives us are not contained within our walls. No, we don't keep the joy all to ourselves. We also strive to make sure every customer with whom we do business experiences the Dillanos Coffee Roasters culture for themselves.

The men and women we serve at Dillanos are also our friends -- our extended family. That's right, family. We don't just sell coffee. We build relationships. We believe it is of the highest priority to provide our family of customers the same kind of commitment and partnership we show to each other and to our own families at home.

It is part of our mission to "Help People." We convey this sense of family by assisting each and every customer in their business endeavors however we can; to give them what they need, even what they want, sometimes even before they are aware they need or want it; to give them yesterday what they would've needed today. Anything less just wouldn't be enough. Besides, it makes coming to work every day a lot more fun.

Part of what makes a family great is the commitment that each one has to the entire group. This gives them the powerful capacity to act as a single unit.

Think of September 11, 2001. If you ask one hundred different people what they remember, you'll probably get one hundred different answers. What sticks out in my mind is witnessing the entire of New York City, with the goodwill of a nation behind it, rallying together and responding as one unit to what could have been its darkest hour. Tragic times, yes. But their single-minded devotion to their city and to each other brought them, and all of us, hope to keep moving forward.

Without boundaries you can grow into anything.

To be wholly defined as successful, a company must show the same kind of devotion to its people, its business partners, humanity and to its product. Every person in the organization must be on board in order for a company to reach its full potential.

> Do whatever it takes to form a lasting relationship with employees and customers.

At Dillanos, we have that same kind of devotion. All of us, from the new guy just starting out bagging beans, up to senior management share the same vision and values. This drives everyone to commit wholeheartedly.

The power this single-mindedness gives us has led to some extraordinary things.

Our CEO and sales and marketing team were investing fast-mounting time, energy and money to land the largest account in Dillanos' history. The challenge was the fact that the potential chain customer was located thousands of miles away in Annapolis, Maryland. It was going to be a challenge, to say the least.

Dillanos flew the owner and five of his café managers to our roaster. Management was running around, urging all of us to be on our toes and treat the guests like family. Here's the core point of this story: We didn't change a thing and the customers absolutely loved our staff.

After a gloves-off blind taste test against the incumbent roaster, CEO, David Morris, started the fun and games. With the teaser of dangling a carrot in front of the tough-to-commit potential customer, David saw the spark in their eyes at the mention of the closing carrot. As the guests were taking a tour of the plant, David dashed to a nearby store, bought a bunch of carrots, hid them back by the roaster, then lured the guests back out to the warehouse and whipped them out from behind a box!

The first real group interaction our guests saw was by sitting in on our staff meeting. You'll read later in the book about Dillanos' outrageously fun staff meetings. The day after the guests flew back to Maryland, our entire staff signed a giant thank you card. It was adorned by a watercolor of carrots painted by our current Sales and Marketing Manager, Keith Hayward, who once was a professional artist. He worked late into the night after they flew home creating this masterpiece. After much correspondence, with many references to a joke someone had made

Just say no to confining job descriptions.

about carrot-dangling, the final message from Maryland read like this, "Carrots help us see things more clearly. Congratulations."

The response was immediate. The entire staff congregated in the lobby and let loose with a round of back patting, cheers and applause.

This is only one example of many that illustrates how we, as a single-unit with the same end in mind, have seemingly moved mountains.

John Berg: Down with Job Descriptions

Let me get my introduction out of the way. I am a driver for Dillanos Coffee Roasters.

Doesn't sound like the most exciting work in the world, does it? How about Mom? Is she bragging to all her friends about her son's great vocational achievement? Mine does!

At first introduction, the title of delivery driver just doesn't sound like you could do that much with it. But before you jump to judgment, I am one delivery guy with some insight on customer care that will hopefully turn your thinking around!

First, when I jotted down that I am a driver at Dillanos, I failed to give you my <u>real</u> role at the company. I serve not only as the main daily contact with customers spread along Puget Sound's I-5 corridor, but I also take on a piece of everybody's job in the company, from head-honcho to sales, warehouse and packaging.

It doesn't matter where you start at a job. What matters is what you do with your position while you're there. To do that, you have to work in a place where there aren't any boundaries, a place where your voice and ideas are as powerful as those of your boss; a place where you never feel your job is threatened by speaking out.

Let's start with the CEO. At least from what I understand, he is the guy who creates bonding relationships with staff and customers.

Now let's look at how far Dillanos' CEO, David Morris, will go to keep a customer relationship alive, healthy and growing.

Winter storms were horrific in February several years ago. Our main source of out of state shipping was on strike and one of Dillanos' customers in Long Beach, California just ran out of coffee for his small chain of specialty coffee cafés. It didn't matter that David had a full agenda and literally dozens of things he had to do. In less than an hour of talking to the terribly worried friend and customer, David took to the wheel of one of Dillanos' delivery trucks in Sumner, Washington. Fourteen hours later he pulled into the customer's parking lot with his weekly delivery.

Go way beyond what's reasonable for your customers. The rich relationship you build is only your first reward.

Even more dramatic, David made this same run a week later.

That small customer is currently Dillanos' largest account. With an aggressive and highly successful franchising program, the chain is growing into hundreds of locations.

What CEO wouldn't have jumped on their horse and rode when their largest customer needed help? The better question is, "What CEO will drop everything and go over-the-top for a small customer?" What an inspiring example of our mission statement.

Again in 2001, around Thanksgiving time, our Roast Master, Phil Beattie, made emergency deliveries to other California customers.

Once again, there we were, racing against the clock.

Braving one of the worst storms slamming the West Coast that winter, Phil ended up leaving around six o'clock on a Friday evening, making deliveries from northern Los Angeles to Santa Monica in the early morning on Saturday and late into the evening. He finally took a rest on Saturday night, only to turn around and drive back through the storms of California and Oregon. Phil made it back in time to clock into work at the roaster early Monday morning.

I understand Phil was met with cheers and a bunch of back patting on Monday morning for living our mission.

While these are just two of our every-week stories that fill Dillanos' history book, the past helps inspire me to exceed the expectations of just another delivery guy. I really get to know and become a friend of every customer I serve.

I try to go beyond what's expected of a normal delivery driver. I am also the customers' daily sales representative. There I am again with that daily smile and questions about their business to make sure we are doing all we can to help them make a buck.

I have only taken you through the many ways my job is so much more than the typical job description. We all cross-train in other departments at Dillanos before settling into the position we have been hired to fill, regardless of immediate demands to fill the job.

I have never worked anywhere else where management will go so far to help each of us understand where we and the person next to us fits into the big picture. It gives you a dignified respect for everyone around you.

By now, you are getting the idea that at Dillanos, nobody is just this or that. We all care the same, which is huge, about each other and our customers.

Okay, I just have to give you one more example of life as a "delivery driver" at Dillanos.

Genuine recognition fuels motivation.

Not long ago, I was delivering coffee to a cart inside an office building. The owner started our conversation out that day by letting me know about the morning's adventures.

While waiting for his coffee, one of her customers noticed a car pulling away from the building that looked just like his. It was!! The owner (Betty) ended up running outside after the car and was the only one who got a close-up look at the thief. Unfortunately, the car thief got away.

In the midst of Betty dramatically retelling this story to me, a police officer came strolling in to let her know that they had caught a suspect a few miles down the road. He said that she was the only one that could identify him.

This posed a difficult decision for Betty. Being a one-person company, she didn't know what to do. To walk away from her cart meant losing a part of the day's profit. At the same time, she felt strongly about nailing this thief who violated her customer.

This is where the example from David's "Right This Minute"

thinking popped into my head. I asked Betty if she would like me to take over so she could go to the police station. That's right; Betty's delivery guy was all of a sudden acting as her support barista staff.

She paused and asked if I really could.

I told her that I had barista training and could confidently run her cart without problems. While I had only served Betty for a couple of weeks, she told me she trusted me and off she went with the officer.

Before they left, the officer promised that it would only take ten to fifteen minutes at the most. After the first fifteen minutes and non-stop customers, I expected them to come back through the door any second.

When the second fifteen minutes came and went, I knew I was in for the long haul. Betty and the officer came back after forty-five minutes with the news that they had

Creativity is limitless when you dissolve all boundaries.

nabbed the right guy and, because of Betty's quick thinking to get a look at the culprit, he was arrested.

Betty was very shocked and delighted to come back and find out that I had non-stop customers from the time she left until the time she got back.

After a gushing apology, hugs and constant thank you for my commitment to her, I felt great! All I could do was smile for the next few days.

By the way, Betty was so grateful that, unbeknownst to me, she called Dillanos and gushed over what I had done to my boss --and even our CEO.

My general manager, Scott, said he swallowed hard at first when a customer called him out of the blue with the opening line, "I need to talk to you about your driver, John!"

Scott said his first thought was, "What could John have done to upset a customer? He <u>never</u> gets bad feedback." Seconds later, Scott's worries were gone. Betty just wouldn't stop flooding him with promises to tell everybody she knew about how great Dillanos is in going the extra mile for even it's smallest customers.

That one-hour of overtime had just created the most powerful extension of our sales imaginable.

I didn't end up finding out about that phone call until our next monthly meeting when Scott told the entire staff that this was what customer service is all about. I can't tell you how much that kind of recognition meant and still means to me.

The examples we get and the recognition we receive is what drives us to push past our own boundaries and achieve goals we never even knew we had.

That one customer experience encouraged me to share the enormous personal and company benefits of going the extra mile for customers. So I started jotting down an outline of a booklet I could pass along to other company drivers.

With tremendous help from my coworkers, we came up with

a formal extra-mile training manual for all Dillanos' drivers. This customer service "Guide for Drivers" helps every existing and new Dillanos' delivery driver understand what the company and our customers expect.

We point out in our booklet that our drivers need to embody the "extra mile" concept and are always be there for the customers' needs, <u>no matter what those needs may be.</u>

Some key points we try to instill in a new employee from the start are:

1. Service with a smile. Everyone has heard this one before, but it's not just a facial expression. They need to know that you are happy to be there for them.

2. Take a personal interest in the people you meet. We're here to build relationships, not just customers. Listen to them and their stories. Don't just show up eager to tell them what happened to <u>you</u> over the weekend. You want people to feel free to talk to you.

3. Be super observant. Pay close attention to everything and try to take care of everything yourself without overstepping your boundaries.

4. Follow through. If you promise anything, take care of it immediately, if not sooner.

5. Gain knowledge about the industry you are in and take pride in it. The more you know, the farther you'll get in business and in life.

6. While on the road or out in public, be the guy that lets others in on the freeway or holds the door open for someone in

a hurry. Always remember that public perceptions are not only of ourselves, but the company we represent as well.

The booklet concludes by stating, "Give the customer what they want before they even know they want it."

10

Be a Meet Lover

By Casey Heyer, Marketing / Special Events

Meetings are indispensable when you don't want to do anything.
-John Kenneth Galbrath

Formula 10:

Make every staff meeting and one-on-one meeting fun, and productivity will double.

Meetings are a necessary evil.

The dreaded long agendas, subtle condescending attitudes, ego trips and glazed-over eyes with heads nodding to the leader's dictates. Right?

Many feel that no matter how much effort and time is spent in a meeting, too many details are hashed over and over with too little coming out of the time invested.

You have heard it all before. In fact, you have probably <u>said</u> this before, "It seems like all I do is sit in meetings. I can't get anything done! We spend all our time talking about things when we could just do them."

As a company grows, so do the number of scheduled meetings. It is just

Make the atmosphere of your meetings a gathering of equal friends, joining together with a common vision and mission in running a business.

99

When agendas are slam packed with topics, the usual result is a lot of scribbling on notepads and too little creative thinking. a reality of life that you feel is unavoidable. Furthermore, meetings usually establish the weekly grudges. Who took credit for an idea or action that some other poor soul really created?

I have pity for the people who sit there nodding their heads and pretending to listen. Meanwhile, their mind is focused on the image of a large piece of duct tape firmly placed over the speaker's mouth.

Most managers and higher-ups can't imagine that a meeting filled with fun and laughter can be anything but wasting precious time. They feel that if laughter is taking place, then all they are doing is goofing around.

Here's a reality tidbit: Without a bit of gut-splitting laughter, the thing that suffers most is accomplishment; not to mention people's job satisfaction and company culture.

If the essence of positive energy and excitement is woven into something as common as meetings, something magical truly happens. People actually enjoy work.

The biggest example of how we turn run-of-the-mill meetings into fun-filled extravaganzas is our monthly staff meetings. I wish you could sit in on one to feel the energy, the joy, the love.

These meetings consist of overall company updates, prize giveaways, games and a chance to get an in-depth lesson of a specific department.

We learn about all our new customers and the marketing tactics we take to get them on board.

After all of the updates, we have a game that usually consists of knowledge of the coffee industry. However, group games vary from "Name That Tune" (picked out on the guitar by staff members) to games themed around holidays. The team that scores the highest in the games receives additional raffle tickets. These raffle tickets increase the

It's all about results, so leave your ego at the meeting room door.

chance of winning the prizes. The goofy, but often useful prizes range from cartoon toilet seat covers to DVD players.

It is an on-going process to keep them fresh month after month. The key is to change them around <u>before</u> they get stagnant.

We look out for each other. We give each other a hard time. And best of all, we're laughing and jabbing the whole time.

All of our gatherings at Dillanos are a meeting of minds to get updates, present ideas and most important, to spark ideas within ourselves.

One person's ideas can completely take another person out

HAVE FUN!

of their "in the box" thinking and trigger amazing brainstorming sessions with innovative ideas.

You don't have to be related to run a family culture company.

For us, we feel that strict dress codes and other such formalities in today's casual Friday approach to business can wrap thinking as tight as a necktie. Anyone who participates in a meeting needs one hundred percent creativity on current issues, not on a wrinkle in your pants or worries about a bad hair day.

Our meetings consciously average from one to three topics for discussion. A lot of issues and proposed actions people put on agendas can be taken care of in a brief conversation with the person charged with the responsibility.

Sticking to a short agenda keeps people from getting sidetracked.

Every person's mind is a goldmine. If a company figures out how to tap that treasure, then every meeting will build on the success of a company.

With the agenda e-mailed to all attending before the meeting, all attendees at Dillanos are required to bring all relevant research and information pertinent to the subjects to be covered.

How many meetings have you suffered through when people come unprepared for the subjects to be covered and even worse, no real action came out of the hour you just invested? You dragged yourself up from your chair uninspired, frustrated and confused on what, if anything, got accomplished.

Meetings at Dillanos are really more like an open forum. Everyone's ideas on the topics are welcomed and often get over-the-head snaps. This is a crazy recent addition where we raise our hands in the air and snap our fingers as a way to congratulate someone. Yes, it's corny. And yes, it's fun. Face it, we are all just kids in grown-up bodies.

No ideas are passed over without consideration by all attendees. We put our personal agendas aside and think about what is best for the company. The magic of expanding on each other's ideas makes for great brainstorming.

Consider seasoning your meeting schedules with mind and thought refreshing field trips.

Leaving your ego at the door has to start with the CEO. The issues and ideas are what matters. And the best way to get those issues taken care of is with a relaxed, uplifting atmosphere.

Ego-driven meetings may create a self-satisfying attentive audience at the moment, but will later lead to resentment and even rebellion on getting tasks completed.

How did Dillanos evolve into a company with meetings more

like family gatherings than employee punishment? It is easy to have a family atmosphere because it is literally a family company.

It seems to me that most people have two different personalities: A work personality and an away-from-work personality. At many companies, a husband or wife would not even recognize their spouse's personalities in

Use your mind and heart when planning and attending meetings.

the work environment. Why should they? At home, everyone is not out to get them.

Creating a creative culture isn't an event or a monthly motivational speaker. It is a lifestyle change that is as simple as bringing your home personality to work.

Regardless of how many employees and departments we add, our fun-loving meetings will never be lost to uptight and rigid gatherings.

It is possible to have a relaxed environment and still have tons of productivity. Everyone is there for each other and holding each other accountable at the same time. Don't think there aren't daily fireworks. What separates us from the crowd is that we are:

- Quick to passionately argue a point
- Quick to forget those fits and outbursts
- Quick to let grudges pass

• Quick to act just like a family

At times, you'll hear the meeting leader bolt out of his/her chair and call out, "Time for a field trip!" Changing our environment adds a new perspective and spices up the monotonous routine of always sharing thoughts in the same spot. Usually the field trip is little more than going to one of the other departments in the building for a time out and zone in on what adventures they are cooking up that day.

Often we shake things up by meeting at a restaurant, a nearby park or go look at a local competitor. There is nothing like a new venue to get the juices flowing, while continuing to build on group camaraderie.

Patterns of thought get established after meeting in the same room week after week. A new environment makes the thought and discussion process fresh and exciting.

You have likely heard the definition of insanity: Do the same thing over and over expecting different results. Meetings are a critically important part of every businessperson's life.

Combine mind and heart in meetings and you will instantly get more productivity and pleasure out of the process than you could ever imagine.

11

Never Settle for an Average Cup of Joe

By Phillip C. Beattie, Roast Master

*Quality is the result of a carefully constructed cultural environment.
It has to be the fabric of the organization, not part of the fabric.*

- Philip Crosby

Formula 11:

Quality Products = Quality Culture

Quality music. Quality vehicles. Quality instant coffee? They don't make them like they used to, do they? Wrong! They do, it just takes some time sorting through a mountain of choices to find genuine quality. In a time when brand choices seem limitless, quality is more important to success than ever before. With the mass media and the Internet, we have become avid rapid-time researchers and connoisseurs.

You know what make, model and features profile the custom car of your dreams. You know the taste attributes of your favorite

> # Knowing what an inferior product is can be your most useful tool to developing a great one.

Merlot, Chardonnay and micro beer. Of course, you know your favorite coffee.

Quality is not always appreciated today, but it is always demanded. Quality is more than a routine check or procedure. Quality is religion.

You may be thinking, "Religion? That's a pretty strong word."

Webster defines religion as "A personal set or institutionalized system of attitudes, beliefs and practices."

That, my friends, is what it takes to achieve quality. It is a never-compromising, religious way of thinking.

Obsessively study the competition.

You may not be directly involved in the coffee industry. But I hope that by outlining the intensive steps that are taken to make a quality cup of coffee, a similar religion of quality will show through in the pride you take in what product or service your company sells.

Developing an understanding of what quality is not, is crucial to setting high standards.

For example, in the coffee industry there is a procedure we go through called "cupping." In a cupping, we taste highly concentrated cups of coffee from a single origin. The coffee is graded based on it's aroma, body, flavor, acidity and aftertaste.

An incredible number of factors go into creating this taste. In fact, from when the

The love/hate search for quality should be endless.

coffee is a seed of a cherry to when it is the rich, full body beverage in your cup, there are over 150 steps that can negatively affect the flavor of the coffee.

With coffee, as with anything, there are defects. Beans that were over ripe when picked. Beans that got wet and fermented. Beans that got insect damage on the tree. And on, and on.

As Dillanos' Roast Master, my critical ingredient to maintaining consistent, perfect quality is being able to recognize even a hint of a defect in the flavor of the coffee.

When I learned how to cup coffee, I tasted a great coffee and a horrible coffee side by side. The good coffee had a rich, smooth, sweetness to it.

> Get every employee on track to reach their full potential as fast as their passion carries them.

While the not-so-good coffee smelled like dirty gym socks. This made the great coffee taste that much more impressive.

In addition, the memory of that defective taste will stay with you for years. Any coffee that has just a hint of that taste will stick out like a sore thumb. I like to refer to this as the "Tequila Effect." One too many shots and you won't want to taste a hint of it again.

This technique can be applied to any business. Seek out your worst and best competitor. It is critical to help redefine "the best."

Most products, if not all, have much more that goes into its creation than the average person could begin to imagine. It is the same with coffee.

The first time I walked through a roasting facility, I was

fascinated by the amount and complexity of work that went into roasting coffee. It was this fascination that spurred me to find out all I could about coffee.

As I began quenching my thirst for coffee knowledge, something stuck out to me. I was not alone in my exploration.

Every person I came in contact with at Dillanos was relentlessly pushing their mental boundaries to reach their full potential.

> Your product's quality is not determined by how much work or money goes into it. It is determined by the response you receive from your customer.

So I had to ask myself, "Why doesn't every company have people with this thirst for information?"

And then it hit me: It is the religion of quality!

Answer this for me: If Dillanos sold the worst coffee in the world, would I have found an atmosphere conducive to learning about coffee? Of course not. All of my findings would have condemned my own work at Dillanos.

Next question: Could Dillanos forge such a satisfying creative culture if the staff believed some competitors sold better products? The culture would crumble faster than a hard cookie.

A passionate commitment to quality is the fuel that energizes Dillanos.

Is it easy to achieve quality? Not always. I can't tell you how many nights I've spent working on the roaster. Crawling out from underneath it at midnight covered in coffee suet, but with a toothy smile plastered on my face.

By daybreak when I taste an absolutely superb cup of coffee, I feel centered in what my working life is all about: A never-ending quest for perfection.

Even better than tasting the coffee is the unsolicited compliments from people who love coffee.

It's just like the credit card commercials...
Two hours working on roaster $200.00
Throwing away a burnt batch of coffee $1,500.00
Knowing you have the best coffee   Priceless

Time for a toast and a boast. A real shootout, western style. Once upon a time, there was a great duel between two powerhouse coffee roasters. Dillanos was pitted against another roaster with a nationally well-known reputation for consistent quality.

We were vying for the business of a sizable chain of east coast specialty coffee shops. They had a nine-year respectful relationship with their current micro roaster. Their first criteria before even remotely considering changing to Dillanos was consistent quality.

We set up the blind taste-off show-down, paying to fly the coffee chain owner and all five of his store managers across the country. We spent a bundle of dough on those plane, hotel and meal tickets. A classic Dillanos adventure!

I brewed up the unidentified coffees one by one. We tasted them head to head, Ethiopian vs. Dillanos' Ethiopian, and so on.

> Belief in the quality of the company as a whole is the foundation for more fulfilled employees.

It seemed to go on for hours. As the coffee grounds settled, the winning coffees stood out tried and true. It was a clean sweep. Dillanos edged out the competition in every category!

The best part of the showdown? Our entire staff planned on winning the blind taste test. You'd better not play without the reality that we know we are the best. As soon as our guests walked out the front doors to return to their hotel, every employee's pride was bouncing off the walls.

The whole time this tasting was happening, was I calm, cool and collected? Not a chance! I was shakin' like a bean in the grinder. There is always that subjective aspect of the word "quality."

It's not that I didn't have confidence in the quality of our coffee. On the contrary. I knew the coffees on the table were exactly how I wanted them to taste. But the truth is, it didn't matter what I thought. The only thing that counted was the customer's opinion.

By the way, they carefully reviewed their evaluation of the tasting and switched to Dillanos. Quality prevailed and so did a boost to our bottom line profit.

I am always looking to tap into other roasters' wisdom and counsel. I was talking with a retired roaster who had years ago worked at a huge, commercial coffee company. It was a great opportunity to soak up war stories and insider information on the big boys.

He shared all sorts of campfire stories that could have been great investigation pieces for the local news. Spoiled, burnt coffees being sold, fires and breakdowns. The stories kept coming. The impression he gave was one of an industrialized production line job, not the art of roasting that I was expecting.

He told me he was just an average nine-to-five Joe who roasted coffee beans for ten years just to pay the bills.

Quality has to be demanded from the top down.

Coffee was no different than a widget. He didn't have an ounce of enthusiasm, let alone passion, for coffee. Just "workin' for the man" to get the paycheck.

It's not that this man had no passion for quality. The pursuit of it was discouraged by the culture of that company. There was no encouragement to increase quality because there was no value placed on it, starting from the owner on down.

In the end, there is something more important than the quality of the coffee. It is the underlying principle in the religion of quality.

It is the awareness and genuine hunger for quality in every aspect of your life.

 **12**

Brother, Can You Spare a Dime?

By Cassie Porcella, Human Resources Manager

We make a living by what we get, we make a life by what we give.
- Sir Winston Churchill

Formula 12:

Make giving back a personal mission with every employee.

There should come a point in every company where the goals of the company shift from being solely profits oriented to being a mix of people and profit.

When a company makes this shift they are able to get a better picture of why they are in business. This does not mean everything will be rosy, but it turns the attention to making positive gains in all aspects of the company.

Now, we've all heard companies talk about their social responsibility or what they give back and to whom. Social consciousness and cause marketing are the buzzwords in defining contributions companies make today.

Shout to the world from the mountaintops what a giving company you are, then rush to your public relations department to spread the good news. "We are the company with a heart."

But you have to ask yourself, is that what it is really about? Do I give just to see my name in lights?

So what makes Dillanos different from others in the context of giving? Attitude. It is all about the attitude. Dillanos, like many other companies, gives money, products and time to charitable causes. Yet we have a greater purpose. We are not just giving for the glory. Any company can get their name in the paper or get a tax deduction by giving.

Don't just give for the recognition; give for the benefit of your soul -- and others.

The focus should be on the good that is being done, rather that on how much is being given, to whom and by whom.

We see hundreds of requests each year asking for donations. Some only ask a bag of coffee to be used at an event, while others need a gift basket for a fundraiser. No matter what they ask, we try to accommodate as many requests as possible.

Beyond the donations, Dillanos is also able to make a difference by being a part of community, national and international causes.

So why do <u>we</u> give, you ask?

We say little, if anything, to the press about our individual and collective giving. We give because it is who we are.

So now that you have a picture of why we give, it is important to see that when Dillanos gives back, it is <u>everyone</u> giving back. It is not just the management or ownership, but every member of the company.

You could say that giving back starts at home (or work). Dillanos' most important contributions are made on behalf of the staff. Each employee at Dillanos is assigned a child to sponsor

Don't be afraid to align yourself with a cause. It helps define who you are corporately and personally.

through the Christian Children's Fund. What was that you say? Sponsoring children? For every staff member? Yes, Dillanos has chosen to include every member of the company in giving and child sponsorship is a great avenue for making giving personal.

Each employee is permanently assigned to a child to whom they can write and send financial contributions. As part of the benefits package, the company fully pays for the sponsorship, but each employee gets the fulfillment of maintaining the relationship. In addition, each child is from a coffee growing region, allowing us to have an even closer connection.

These kids' names are not just drawn out of a hat. They come from areas in the world that provide our livelihoods. The true meaning of giving back is supporting those who support you, whether they are in your community, state or across the world.

Giving back on behalf of your employees not only says that the cause is important, but also reinforces the importance of the employee. Our staff already gives a large amount of their personal time to causes such as youth groups, charities and local sports and recreation.

Because our staff has more than an average share of twenty and thirty-somethings, it would be hard for most to also financially support important causes. By allowing staff to have the benefits of supporting a child and giving back, Dillanos enhances our self-worth and loyalty to the company.

My first personal experience with the true culture of giving at Dillanos came right after I started working at Dillanos on September 10, 2001. The next day, everyone was stunned by the shocking events at the World Trade Center and the Pentagon. Imagine my surprise when our Chairman of the Board, Howard, came in and said that if anyone wanted to donate blood, they could take a paid hour to do so. As a new employee, I was impressed by the quick and selfless response to the

Be an employer that is willing to more than partner with your staff in the effort to give.

situation. Just being given the opportunity to give back made me feel great about my job, and even better about being a part of the company.

After seeing this from the company in my first week on the job, the thought crossed my mind, "Is there anything that can top that display?" I can honestly say that there have been many situations since then that have shown me just how much Dillanos cares.

Above even that, I have seen that each employee is encouraged to use his or her gifts to make giving a personal commitment.

For example, our team at Dillanos participates in non work-related community events. In the summer of 2003, Dillanos started working with the American Cancer Society's Relay for Life. One of our sales reps, Anna, put together a team to walk in the relay and raise money to find a cure for cancer. Many of our staff responded to the call and walked in the relay as part of "Team Dillanos," all because they felt personally led to participate.

Make giving real by management setting a personal example beyond corporate cash and time contributions.

The participation among the staff was great and the team was able to help others in the relay by serving hot coffee for the overnight event. Dillanos also began selling a special Hope Blend through the American Cancer Society with the proceeds going to the Society's efforts to cure cancer. Why is this cause so important to us? Because many of the staff at Dillanos have been touched by cancer in one way or another.

Since we are a family at Dillanos, if something affects one of us, it affects all of us. By taking such an active role in the fight against cancer, it allows us all to be apart of the cure.

The holiday season brings out giving at every level at Dillanos. The company, staff and even our customers get into the spirit of the season by focusing on giving to worthy causes.

In partnership with our customers, Dillanos sells our "It's A Wonderful Blend" coffee, with proceeds going to help the U.S. Marines' Toys for Tots program. Though a relatively new undertaking for Dillanos, in the holiday seasons that we have been producing the blend, it's popularity with customers has grown immensely. Our customers purchase the coffee to sell in their establishments as a way for their customers to give back to the community. And each year we present an award to the shop or stand that has contributed the most.

So the question remains, how do you make giving a personal commitment for every employee?

The first key to make giving real is by setting the example. If your company is not willing to give, your staff won't be willing either. Setting the example and maintaining the company's commitments will transform the culture.

Make giving a team effort that involves everyone. When your staff feels included in company giving, they will be willing to get involved and commit to the cause.

Most importantly, make it easy for your staff to give. Keep your staff informed about charitable opportunities that arise. Also, give the freedom that is necessary for your staff to pursue outside giving-related commitments.

If your staff does not respond right away, be patient. When they see the solid commitment from the top of the organizational chart, they'll feel more comfortable in taking part.

THERE IS NO "I" IN SALES

By Jeff Woods, Director of Sales

Alone we can do so little: together anything is possible.
-Helen Keller

Formula 13:

Always make getting customers a team effort.

Just about every business uses the tired phrase, "Sales is what drives the company." It's what sales reps with huge egos love to hear. It's what keeps them motivated - always hungry for the next pat on the back from the CEO.

Unfortunately, it's also what keeps those sales reps ostracized from the rest of the company! No production employee wants to hear about the newest notch on sales reps' post. It only translates into a larger workload for them to produce, causing resentment and separation between sales and fulfillment.

Time to shift that sales-first mentality.

In our case, it's the COMPANY that drives our sales. As much as we'd love to, our sales department cannot take credit for the growth we've incurred over the years. Although we have been blessed with yearly sales increases averaging nearly 30%, our success can only be attributed to the fact that this company, and everyone in it, offers immediate buy-in value to anyone who visits us.

By now, you've read about the ownership every Dillanos employee takes over their positions in our company. That's a big part of equation. We may only have eight sales reps, but with everyone in the company buying into the goal of Helping People, Making Friends, and Having Fun, we have 70+ team members, all working towards the same cause.

After meeting up with a huge potential customer at an Atlanta Coffee Fest trade show, our sales rep, Ryan, invited the potential customer and his wife to fly out to Seattle to visit our roaster. This being Ryan's first "big lead," he was overly anxious to make the perfect impression with this perspective customer.

Not to miss any opportunity to blow the customer away, Ryan planned every detail of their visit; from picking them up and escorting them around in a brand new Escalade, to securing a choice hotel room with easy access to downtown Seattle for a convenient vacation in the downtime.

Ryan also met with all the department managers to make sure every employee was ready to put the extra "wow" factor into their very first tour of our facilities.

When the day came for their visit, every department got on board and answered the call of duty:

· Every inch of our warehouse was spotless.

· We had a customized welcome sign in the front lobby, created by our graphic design team ready to greet them.

· Phil, our Roast Master, had prepared a private cupping, tailored specifically to match their flavor profiles.

· Our marketing team had a visual presentation, outlining our enhanced brand program for their upscale cafes.

Make your whole team ready and willing to add value to all new business presentations.

· I, along with the rest of our executive team, was ready with a revised business action plan, designed to increase their profits through structured future development.

· The customer service department was ready to greet them and explain the nature of our weekly order process, designed to maintain peak freshness and quality.

The WHOLE team was ready and willing to add value. We were all eagerly awaiting our turn to show the customer why we loved working for Dillanos, and why we were certain they'd love working with us, too!

Of course, with all that careful planning and effort, we were all expecting the end result to be nothing short of a triumphant victory. What we weren't expecting was the reason WHY they decided to partner with us.

Days later, Ryan and I had a conversation with David, the owner of the company we were courting and newest addition to the Dillanos family. After expressing his appreciation for all the details that we had planned out with precision, he said the one thing that stuck in his mind about the company was his unplanned interaction with a coffee packager named Brett.

During the tour, David explained, Brett took David away from the scheduled procession through the warehouse to give him a hands-on response to his question about customized retail packaging and our ability to provide solutions for his future retail needs.

Rather than answering with a simple, "Yes, we can do that," Brett opened up a finished container of pre-portioned coffee packets to allow David a chance to see and smell the freshness and quality that our special pack design offered. Brett explained that the design of our portion bags allows us to package the coffee immediately after it's roasted, rather than having to wait a couple days for its gasses to be fully released. He showed David the pack's one-way valve that allowed the gasses in the coffee to be released during transit so he could take delivery of the coffee much

Have fun in everything you do, even cold sales calls.

sooner than if he had waited for the off-gassing to finish before sealing the packs (as is typical practice).

Although the idea of retail portion packaging was only a minor concern of his, David was blown away by the passion Brett exuded for his role at creating the ultimate customer experience. If Brett, a warehouse worker, has this much love for his job with Dillanos, David thought, this company must be the real deal.

Yes, we were able to get him in the door with our sales rep, woo him over with marketing, and impress him with a commitment to coffee quality, but what really won him over was the authenticity of something completely unplanned - the dedication of an employee with true buy-in.

To offer another perspective on the subject, Anna Gutierrez, our Southeast Territory Leader, recalls a team story from early on in her career with Dillanos.

As most of you in sales have experienced, it can be a very discouraging profession, especially if it's a one-man job. "I'm even guilty of being the sellee who hates solicitors knocking on my door or calling my phone at home," Anna explains.

"A lot of the time, I have an idea or intuition of what's going through a potential customer's mind by reading their body language and often humorous 'stay away' facial expressions. The standard first words out of the person's mouth are, 'Sorry, I'm not interested.' That's when the fun of sharing what's unique about Dillanos begins.

"Even though persistence can drive a prospective customer (and me!) a bit crazy, most of the time it's the only way to scale huge goals and to let your leads know you're positive about the results they'll get with your partnership."

Early in her career, Anna met some potential customers (now current customers and friend of Anna's) at an annual specialty coffee trade show in Seattle. "I love Dillanos" was all she needed to read on their comment sheets after sampling our coffee. Talk about a huge buying signal! Anna needed to act fast if she was to capitalize on the positive Dillanos experience with this successful coffee business.

She began visiting their business and through the next few weeks, started to develop a great relationship with the owner, manager, and baristas. As great of a job she was doing to be the ambassador of Dillanos to them, she still fell short of being able to sell them on the benefits of her company without some help.

Good or bad, your company culture will set the tone for a sale.

Normally, we would find a way to introduce our perspective customers to the rest of the team through a tour at our roaster. This gave us a chance to show the benefits of our resources, our support, and the buy-in we all have with this company. Every Dillanos sales rep knows that once people see and experience our culture, ninety percent of the time it's the first day in a long relationship! No matter how hard she tried, however, Anna just couldn't seem to get them to tour Dillanos.

At our weekly sales meeting, we all came together to brainstorm a plan that would resolve a way to overcome their reluctance to come to us. As with every sales meeting, we had access to the top sales minds in the company. From our administrative assistant up to our CEO, we all were able to put our creative talents together to come up with a solution. And it worked!

The day finally came when they tugged open our front door and were greeted with VIP treatment from our staff. Knowing what it took to get these customers into our doors, we all made an extra effort to help Anna close the deal. Our entire team was poised to create the ultimate star experience for them as soon as they walked into our roaster. The buy-in was there from the moment we all put our heads together, and we weren't going to let this one slip through our fingers!

Soon after the tour, Anna took both of our vice presidents and our roast master to visit their specialty coffee retail location to discuss over lunch the similar visions we shared with our businesses. While the objective was to close the deal, even after two meetings with several members of our team, they still were somewhat reluctant to make the move to Dillanos. She knew the relationship we had built up to that point was something rare, and she was sure they needed to be adopted into the Dillanos family. But, you can't force someone to make even the best decision until they're ready for it.

Now, most sales reps may have given up by this stage in the game, but not Anna, and not her team at Dillanos. Her obsession with making this partnership happen was infectious. WE wouldn't let her give up on them!

Finally, about a week later, Anna secured another meeting

with her customer. This time, she brought our CEO, David, along with Keith, Vice President of Sales and Marketing, knowing full well that when David and Keith put their sights on something, they find a way to make it happen!

They went over to that meeting with the goal of not leaving their place with the word, "No."

We all knew we were the best fit for each other. They were the best Dillanos customer we didn't have, and they agreed we were the best coffee roaster they didn't have! Needless to say, David and Keith helped Anna leave with a "Yes," and one of the greatest examples of how our Dillanos family works together as a team.

By now you've learned how these examples of teamwork have made such a successful impact on the growth of Dillanos.

Mindy Schaneman, Northwest Territory Leader, best puts this concept into perspective.

"After closing a sale, the entire team really comes into play in our business. All departments play a role in customer retention. It's the combined efforts from our roast master roasting the best product possible, customer service taking orders, the packaging department labeling and packing the product, the shipping department getting the customer exactly what they ordered, and back to the sales department maintaining a good relationship with the customer."

Imagine how much longer you can hold onto an account if each department team member feels as though they play a vital nurturing role in the business.

The buy-in value for each employee plays out directly into the value perceived by your potential and current customers. Investing into a culture that provides this buy-in will allow you to harness the closing and retention power of your entire team.

 **Conclusion**

After all this verbiage we have given you, what you really need now is time. Time to think.

Jump into RTM (Right This Minute) and give yourself a few minutes right now to grade how your company measures up to Dillanos' thirteen formulas to forging a creative culture.

Let go of those instant pop-up thoughts of staff members who resist change and those "can't do" fears that can start creeping up your spine and freeze your mind.

After you circle an honest grade on the chart on the next page, don't get hung up on rationalizing why you circled a C or even a D. Start believing in your power to change everything to an A. Every change starts and ends with a belief so deep down in your soul that nobody can shake your absolute certainty that you can create a great company. All turn-arounds are a turn around in absolute beliefs.

Most people focus on what they are afraid of, instead of what can be. It all begins with your imagination, free of conventional management ideas and open to the rewards of forging a self-expressive culture that celebrates individuality and crystal clear common goals.

135

Start right now thinking and acting like your company is already living Dillanos' thirteen formulas for success.

Every staff member at Dillanos can testify that you will feel so good, that your staff and customers will instantly recognize the contagious energy and begin craving it on a daily basis.

Think about how you want the halls and offices in your company to feel the instant you walk through the door. Life is nothing but emotions -- starting with yours.

Like exercise, the hardest part is taking that first step. Having the courage and self-confidence to begin your life and your company on a brand new adventure every day is contagious.

There is such a joy in liberating and celebrating each other's success. Soon, you'll find that every member of your staff will start showing up at the office each day giving the best that they can give.

Take that first step to creating a fantastic company by honestly circling your grade to see how your company sizes up to Dillanos' thirteen formulas for *Brewing A Creative Culture*.

Formula 1
Hire from the heart for the heart.
A   B   C   D   F

Formula 2
Live by extremes in fun and discipline, with the power of personal ownership and empowerment bouncing off the walls.
A   B   C   D   F

Formula 3
Make the speed of accomplishment a game everybody wants to play.
A   B   C   D   F

Formula 4
Be honest in all things, even when no one is looking.
A   B   C   D   F

Formula 5
While education can be important, potential fit within your culture is what matters most.
A   B   C   D   F

Formula 6
Celebrate each other's successes.
A   B   C   D   F

Formula 7
Make your business a "family" business.
A   B   C   D   F

Formula 8
Keep the curiosity, wonder and freshness of youth alive in everybody.
A   B   C   D   F

Formula 9
Make an over-the-top commitment to customers.
A   B   C   D   F

Formula 10
Make every staff meeting and one-on-one meeting fun, and productivity will double.
A   B   C   D   F

Formula 11
Quality Products = Quality Culture
A   B   C   D   F

Formula 12
Make giving back a personal mission with every employee.
A   B   C   D   F

Formula 13
Always make getting the customers a team effort.
A   B   C   D   F

About the Authors

Brewing a Creative Culture was written by select management and staff members of the Dillanos Coffee Roasters staff in Sumner, Washington. Growing at record speed, the largest specialty coffee micro roaster in the Northwest is recognized nationally as a business cultural icon by best selling author Jack Canfield, co-author of *Chicken Soup For The Soul* series, and *The Success Principles: How to Get from Where You Are to Where You Want to Be.*

139

Printed in the United States
107287LV00002B/139-240/P

9 781420 833928